BUSES

YEAR BOOK 1992

BUSES
YEAR BOOK 1992

Edited by STEWART J. BROWN

LONDON

IAN ALLAN LTD

CONTENTS

First published 1991

ISBN 0 7110 1992 4

Published by Ian Allan Ltd, Shepperton, Surrey; and printed by Ian Allan Printing Ltd at their works at Coombelands in Runnymede, England.

Front cover:
London Transport's BL9, a Bristol LH6L with ECW bodywork is seen at Stanmore on 26 July 1990 whilst working route 251.   *D. Trevor Rowe*

Rear cover, top:
Bristol VRT EJO 492V is operated by PMT and is seen here unloading at Wolverhampton bus station on 20 July 1990 whilst operating service 545.   *Chris Morrison*

Rear cover, bottom:
Hastings & District were operating this Mercedes L608D on 20 March 1989 and it is seen at Langney, Eastbourne on route 19A.
P. R. Gainsbury

Previous page:
There are not too many customers on this rural bus splashing towards Edinburgh as the snow melts around it. The bus is a Seddon Pennine with Alexander Y-type body, standard fare for Scottish Bus Group subsidiary Eastern Scottish in the late 1970s.   *John Burnett*

Multi-modal in Man

Peter Rowlands *goes in search of the essential character of the Isle of Man and comes back stunned by the richness and variety of its landscape and its transport.*

DAY 1: MORNING

People who fly to the Isle of Man get picked up when they arrive. The cheerful main concourse at Ronaldsway Airport bustles briefly with welcomes; then travellers, friends and relatives drift out to their cars, leaving calm in their wake.

I saunter towards the exit, unwilling to be rushed. To the side of the terminal building an ageing Bedford SB coach mops up remaining passengers. Like me, it's bound for Douglas, seven miles north; but its air of contained bonhomie is unprepossessing. It's for people not interested in where they are.

So I find myself virtually alone on a bench outside the main entrance, watching through a light drizzle for a bus. The timetable says they leave for Douglas every half hour, but the lack of

Below:
Isle of Man Transport has two batches of Northern Counties-bodied Leyland Olympians. The newer vehicles were delivered in 1990 and to reduce glare have shallower windscreens of the style normally fitted to Northern Counties lowheight bodies.

Above:
The island's first Northern Counties-bodied Olympians had standard deep windscreens. A 1989 bus hurries along the Promenade in Douglas.

traffic is not encouraging. It's hard to imagine that buses run here at all.

Across an abundant flowerbed is a curious, green-bronze sculpture – three legs extended like spokes from a wheel. It is a motif I shall see many times before I leave. Nearby a union flag hangs limply from a mast. In spite of it, I have a strange sensation of being abroad. What is the essential quality of Man? Can a long weekend here provide a reviving break from routine?

My fears are unfounded. Almost exactly on time, a cream and red Leyland Olympian of Isle of Man Transport hoves into view. It's on route 1, which seems rather appropriate. I feel revived and impressed. It's one of the latest Northern Counties-bodied examples, looking nearly new. The journey is scheduled to take around half an hour for just over £1 (English money accepted). It seems a bargain. We swing out onto a short stretch of dual carriageway (possibly the only stretch on the island, I later find).

The journey is more tantalising than revealing. Farms, fields, petrol stations, distant mountains. The driver adopts a brisk pace. The roads are reasonably good though hilly and not too wide, the many trees meticulously lopped. The main excitement comes soon after the airport in the village of Balsalla. Here there is a level crossing over the single-track Isle of Man Steam Railway. No trains are in view, but another Olympian looms up at a stomach-churning rate. At the last moment our driver checks his enthusiasm and halts abruptly to let the other squeeze past.

Douglas, the capital, is bigger than you might expect (the other towns are correspondingly smaller). The bus approaches it through leafy suburbs, then climbs narrow Victorian streets to descend steeply through the centre to the sea front. There are shops, traffic, bustle, banks, and a bus station just round the corner, close to the harbour and the ferry terminal.

DAY 1: AFTERNOON

They'll do you a go-anywhere season ticket at the bus station, valid on trams and trains as well as buses. It's good value, especially for seven days; the island's 31 miles by 11 contain as much of transport interest as you're likely to find anywhere in such a small space. You even get a refund on your trip from the airport. You also get a timetable of all the island bus services, which is nicely laid out and includes maps and tourist information. But the page on the history of the island's buses bears the hallmarks of an over-zealous enthusiast. What's a PS1 or a PD1? You're supposed to know this already.

The one thing the go-anywhere ticket isn't valid on is the horse trams that run along the promenade – presumably because they're operated by Douglas Corporation. The sullen conductor explains this irritably and without apology, as though it were obvious: a piece of information evidently delivered often (though not clear from the ticket). This year it costs 60p. The good news is that because of today's rain they're running proper enclosed cars, not the usual toastracks.

The tram clip-clops and rumbles along. People who are not obviously tourists seem to use it routinely, crossing the wide road to the tram

Above:
Douglas Corporation's horse trams started in 1876. The most modern vehicle in the fleet is this enclosed car, dating from 1913.

tracks with practised care. In pictures the trams look small and quaint; in the metal they are quite heavy and substantial, although much is made in publicity about their roller bearings (which make life easier for the 60 horses that maintain the service). In spite of the modern traffic around them, they really do give a feel for what horse trams must have been like when they ran in earnest a hundred years ago.

INTERLUDE: DOUGLAS BUSES

The bus station in Douglas is a neat but undistinguished affair, with bays set out in saw-tooth pattern. I was hoping to photograph some of the second-hand Atlanteans that formed the staple of the fleet for so many years; but after delivery of three batches of new Olympians, these already seem to hold sway.

The first six were bodied by Leyland at Workington in 1988, the remaining 13 by Northern Counties. These came in two batches – the latter with shallower windscreens to reduce the glare experienced with the low driving position. They're all so clean that it's impossible to tell by appearance which came first. The inscrutable Isle of Man numberplates, of course, reveal nothing.

The 80-strong fleet is in the midst of a livery change from cherry red and white to a brighter red and cream. The single-deckers (nearly all Nationals) are in the old livery, the double-deckers mostly in the new. However, the occasional ex-Merseyside Atlanteans seem to be in the old colours, or else in rather garish all-over advertising liveries.

The sea front is a more fertile ground for action pictures – except that the buses are not all that frequent (the main promenade service is only half-hourly). But when you do see one across the horseshoe bay, you have ample time to plan your shot. They proceed slowly and stop frequently, and there's nothing to block your view.

Below:
The first Leyland Olympians for Isle of Man Transport had Workington-built Leyland bodies.

Above:
There are two Leyland Lynxes in the fleet. One passes the Railway Hotel, near Douglas station.

DAY 2: MORNING

The promenade at Douglas is two miles long – further than you'd want to walk very often. Much of it is fronted by ornate Victorian terraces (mostly hotels). The horse trams run the length of it, but I feel wary of the crews' surly demeanour; also obstinately resentful of paying another fare. Anyway, the weather's changed for the better, and a fitful sun is shining; so I end up walking the full two miles. At the northern end, just below a concrete excrescence called Summerland, is the terminus of what many people come to the island to see – the Manx Electric Railway.

The cars tower over those on the horse tramway. In today's sunshine each is pulling an open-sided trailer – although the motor cars, with their vestibule doors and upholstered seats, have a more authentic tramlike air about them. The car jerks into motion and starts the climb up from Derby Castle to the clifftop.

From the start, tramway sensations engulf you. The screech of the wheels against the check rails, the swish of the collector on the wire, the moan of the electric motor, the rattle of the windows in their ill-fitting frames. And the green poles that support the overhead: strange, but they seem more quintessentially tram-like than almost anything else about the journey.

The initial climb alongside the main road gives a taste of what is to come – a stunning view over Douglas bay. As it progresses, the journey is so breathtaking that the reality of it is genuinely hard to grapple with. The leafy-lane landscape, the clifftop vistas are a joy in their own right; but seeing them from this living museum-piece gives the experience an extraordinary piquancy. It's hard to know what to marvel at most.

Sometimes the track follows the road, sometimes it dives off through woodland hedges, past cottage gardens. It constantly crosses and re-crosses the road, and on each occasion the driver sounds the whistle, barely hesitating as he does so. Local motorists clearly know what to expect.

The tramway – or 'interurban', to use the more correct American term – runs north out of Douglas and along the coast to the picturesque village of Laxey, then onward to Ramsey at the north end of the island. It was built in the 1890s, and all surviving cars date back to 1903 or before. It was always intended to attract tourists, and nowadays that is its main function.

It's a juddering, squealing ride, and every piece of the varnished wooden panelling seem to move independently of every other. The full 17-mile ride to Ramsey takes an hour and a quarter. But it's a journey quite utterly without compare, and the presence of modern-day traffic detracts nothing from it. The guide book says the Manx Electric Railway is one of the wonders of the world. I wouldn't dispute it.

DAY 2: LUNCH TIME

Laxey station is an enchanted glen. The village is set in a steep-sided cove: moorland and clifftops above, abundant foliage below. The tram tracks curve across a bridge with stone parapets, then into a tree-lined clearing. The sense of time-warp is complete.

A 1977 Leyland National in the maroon and white livery which is being replaced by a brighter red and cream. In the background a horse plods along with a tram.

Here the Snaefell Mountain Railway veers off. In theory it's a branch of the main line, but in fact it uses different rolling stock and the track gauge is wider (to give more stability).

If the Electric Railway itself is quaint, the Snaefell branch is quite mad – a Victorian tramway that strikes out over totally unpopulated moorland, and continues until it reaches the top of Man's highest mountain (2,036 ft). Mad, but utterly compelling.

What *is* a mountain railway? It conjures up pictures of rack-and-pinion drive and 45-degree ascents. In fact this is nothing like that. At a glance its special trams look much like the others on the system, and they proceed in an approximately horizontal plane. But the track does climb, and steeply, and the pace is slow.

Between the running tracks is an elevated rail, double-headed and placed on its side. Horizontal wheels under the trams bear against this for lateral stability, and in the past auxiliary brake shoes gripped it during the descent. Nowadays rheostatic braking has relieved the need for them. The precautions are reassuring, because the view on the starboard side is hair-raising – a deepening chasm that would make even sheep insecure.

The car moans its way steadily up the side of a hill, past Lady Isabella (the giant waterwheel) and out into moorland. Sunlight dapples the varnished seats. Every minute brings a mounting sense of the surreal. Inside, an Edwardian cocoon

of animated chatter; outside, an empty landscape of moorland and sky. The journey is an impossibility, a dream.

Presently we halt at the mountain road where the Isle of Man TT race passes; then onward and most of the way round the Snaefell peak, still climbing. At the top is a café – welcoming, but drab without the castellations that once adorned it. From here, a short climb on foot leads up to the summit, from where you're supposed to be able to see all the countries of the United Kingdom, and Ireland as well. Scotland seems to be in view today; elsewhere the horizon is lost in haze.

INTERLUDE: RAMSEY BUSES

From Laxey, the main tramway runs on another ten miles or so to the small town of Ramsey on the north coast of the island. The terrain is as stunning as before, but by this stage you're beginning to suffer from landscape overload. The descent through the suburban Ramsey hinterland is almost a relief.

It's a fishing town with tourism tacked on, like many on the island. Its real character is presumably in view, but curiously submerged. It's on the TT route – a fact underlined by the otherwise redundant footbridge over one of the main roads out. Nearby is the bus garage – an impossibly clean pitched-roof structure, painted cream with red relief to match the buses and looking altogether rather like a birthday cake.

Northern Counties Olympians and Nationals hurry past, completing journeys that started in Douglas or Peel. Smart, of course, but their familiarity denies them any special sense of place.

I return to the station for the clattering journey back.

DAY 2: MORNING

If you think the Electric Railway gives you a rough ride, wait till you try the Steam Railway. The track, reportedly in its best condition for years, undulates in a way that makes the tramlines seem like plate glass by comparison. The jarring lateral movement is exhausting. Take a window seat, and by the end of the 15-mile journey your shoulder will ache from being banged against the side.

Yet the smells, the sounds and the sights of the steam journey are compelling. The landscape is not as dramatic as in the north, but the swirling smoke and the strain of the gradients compensate. Four immaculate Victorian side tanks pull the trains, and the coaches (many over 80 years old) are also beautifully restored.

The line runs south from Douglas, the sole remnant of what once was an extensive island network. It's the longest narrow-gauge railway in Britain, and as with the tramway, its very existence has a dreamlike quality. Its only drawback is that its faintly festive air makes it less convincingly utilitarian.

The southern terminus is Port Erin – a small Victorian resort perched over a bay. Comparisons inevitably press themselves on you; this town is like a corner of elegant Eastbourne transplanted to Southwold. But for late summer there are too many vacancy signs.

INTERLUDE: PORT ERIN BUSES

The bus route from Douglas terminates in the railway station yard: a trip taking little more than half the train time, but perhaps offering less to the pioneer spirit. A Northern Counties Olympian stands waiting.

A man is washing a Leyland National. Obligingly he pauses while I photograph it. He should have been off on a works outing, he tells me; only today was a duty day. And where has the outing gone? By train and tram to Laxey and Ramsey, with vintage buses making the connection in Douglas. A busman's holiday *par excellence*; yet he seems genuinely chagrined to have missed it. He commends a video of the island's tramway; regrets that he's loaned his copy to a friend, or I could have borrowed it.

Is this cheery goodwill the essential quality of Man? Or have I merely stumbled on one of life's truly generous souls? Uncertain, I leave him with his hose, and round the corner I catch the photograph of the day: two ex-Merseyside Atlanteans in the new livery.

DAY 2: AFTERNOON

One of the first stops back after Port Erin is Castletown – a compact urban centre with quaint,

Below:
Ramsey bus garage.

inconceivably narrow streets radiating from a square on top of a hill. Here motorcyclists, omnipresent on the island, have gathered in strength for a vintage rally. Matchless and Rudges parade alongside the latest multi-cylinder Hondas. The square is a sea of black leather, yet the suppressed threat of the mainland bike brigade is absent. The cycles, when they're revved up, produce a rumble rather than a roar.

Full-sized buses pick their way through the town, skirting the castle but braving the cramped town square. I watch an Olympian on the now-familiar route 1 as it hurries past.

The last train back is crowded. I share a compartment with two couples. The older pair are on holiday – their twentieth on the island. The other two are natives, and bemoan the lack of investment in the tourist trade.'Guess what our latest attraction is,' the young wife says. 'The DIY centre on the outskirts of Douglas. That's where everyone goes on a Sunday afternoon.' On bus route 1, no doubt. Their children fret as they peer out of the window, unaware of the privilege of being able to make such a journey.

DAY 3: MORNING

There's some kind of motorbike race on today, so the bus from Douglas to Peel (on the far side of

Below:
A 20-year-old Leyland Atlantean/Alexander, acquired from the Merseyside Passenger Transport Executive in the early 1980s, in the latest Isle of Man Transport livery.

the island) is diverted. No problem; it prompts the driver of the newly-acquired Lynx (one of two bought from stock) to press on with gusto. He hurries past fields, moorland, picturesque reservoirs. The landscape changes quickly as we progress.

Approaching St John's, an inland village on the main road, the driver sounds the horn several times and draws to a stop. After a pause, three or four people break hesitantly away from a bus stop some yards off and drift over. 'I don't know,' the driver mutters acerbically, 'they do this trip every day and yet they don't know their own bus.'

They're confused because we've arrived from the wrong direction – something they confirm as they board. 'I heard there was a race on,' the first woman confesses. 'I just forgot about it.' They all seem familiar with the driver and greet him cheerily. He takes their fares and checks their passes with gruff amiability.

St John's is one of the jewels in the island's crown – a slight village in itself, but set in a glorious valley reminiscent of the glens around Pitlochry. After it, Peel's steep cramped streets seem an anticlimax, although it has its quaintness too. It's another fishing town, and less touristy than most. There's an air of Cornwall about it – even something Mediterranean, perhaps. It almost comes as a surprise that Kodacolor film costs the usual price.

INTERLUDE: PEEL BUSES

Yes, well it comes as no surprise to find that Peel buses are exactly the same as Port Erin buses, Ramsey buses, Douglas buses and everywhere else buses. Not just the same type but the same buses. You probably saw them yesterday somewhere else. The red and cream fleet seems to penetrate everywhere, reminding you perhaps more powerfully than anything else that you're on an island. There are local routes, of course – especially around Douglas – but it's commonplace for the same vehicles to strike out on quite long cross-country journeys.

At Peel they hide themselves in a cramped but neat garage hard against the small town centre – as ready for a hike up to Ramsey as for a plod round Douglas bay. 'Before 6pm please wait for your bus in the garage,' a sign instructs you. Why? Back-packers ignore it and squat in the sun.

DAY 3: LUNCH TIME

There's a restless, capital-city quality to the traffic on Douglas promenade. Late into the night it still flows past the Gaiety Theatre. This is where to

Above:
There are six cars on the Snaefell Mountain Railway and all date from 1895. Car 5 was rebodied in original style in 1971, after being damaged.

come if islands make you uneasy. At lunch time things are calmer, but there's still a businesslike briskness about the place. You can see why the Dickensian horse-tram crews become dour.

The hotel receptionist who takes my money is amused that anyone should come to Man to see its transport. Perhaps she's missed the obvious; but perhaps the authorities could be doing even more to promote the extraordinary array of ancient and modern transport systems that run here.

Back at the bus station for the last time, I finally get a picture of an Atlantean in action in the new livery (albeit on a private hire). Then, to set the seal on the proceedings, another one rolls in for the journey back to airport. The hard-working sound of the 680 engine orchestrates the climb out of Douglas and on to Balsalla and Ronaldsway.

Arriving early for the flight, I'm left with time to photograph more buses outside the terminal – in sunshine this time – and to reflect on this place that boasts palm trees, cheap postage, pound notes and three-legged men. What memories will I carry from it? Clean buses? A total lack of minibuses? Arcades on the promenade or immaculate Victoriana everywhere?

All of it, probably, and scenery evocative of so many other places while remaining true to itself. But the personality that endures is that of the brisk bus driver diverted round St John's, and the picture engraved indelibly in my memory is of the sun-splashed Milnes tram of 1895, gamely plodding its pointless, glorious path through emptiness to the top of a mountain.

Below:
A National in the current livery pulls out of Douglas bus station.

W is for War

Roy Marshall recounts the story of the
Karrier/Sunbeam W-type trolleybus._

At the outbreak of World War 2 in September 1939 a number of operators were still in the process of extending trolleybus operation including further conversions of tramway routes.

Cardiff Corporation had still to begin and had the distinction of receiving trolleybuses to virtually pre-war specification with Northern Counties bodywork built alongside utility bodywork on motorbuses. Other operators needed to replace ageing stock or augment their fleets to cater for increased traffic. Some seaside resorts were able to either sell or loan surplus vehicles to urban operators and a number of chassis or complete vehicles intended for South African operators were diverted to the home market but it

was obvious that production of a wartime trolleybus was required.

This resulted in the Rootes' subsidiary Sunbeam situated in Wolverhampton producing the 'W'; a four-wheeler which was normally offered with an 85hp motor by BTH. Despite the hostilities badge engineering was allowed with some chassis carrying Karrier badges and some electrical equipment Metrovick. Karrier had been a member of the Rootes' group for some years and

Below:
Darlington Corporation received 24 wartime single-deckers from Karrier. They entered service in 1943 and 1944 and had centre-entrance Brush bodies. The Karrier badge is just visible above the fleet number.

Above loft:
Doncaster Corporation received nine W-types with bodies by Brush and, as shown here, Park Royal. While the driver opens his windscreen the conductor struggles with the trolley poles. Doncaster's Ws were later rebodied by Roe.

Left:
Hull Corporation's streamlined livery softens the angular lines of the Brush body on this Sunbeam W. Note the Corporation Transport fleetname which assumes, reasonably enough, that everyone already knows they are in Hull.

Above:
Twelve Sunbeam Ws were delivered to Belfast Corporation in 1945 with locally-built Harkness bodywork. The triangular Sunbeam badge is fitted neatly at the base of the windscreen.

trolleybus production had been transferred alongside that of Sunbeam.

Similarly both BTH and Metropolitan-Vickers were part of the AEI group. Although not publicised some equipments were supplied by both EEC and GEC, the former including motors of 115hp. I recall those of this power which were fitted to a small batch of Ws in my home city of Nottingham and which were driven uphill at a speed far in excess of the capabilities of anything else in the fleet. Some vehicles were supplied with battery manoeuvring equipment, a useful facility when stranded on a section insulator as well as enabling the vehicle to turn or deviate very short distances after roads were obstructed by bomb damage.

The first Ws were delivered early in 1943; initially with 56-seat bodywork constructed by both Weymann and Park Royal and with a 33-seat central entrance single-decker by Brush. The earliest double-deckers had leatherette upholstery and a completely panelled emergency door; this later gave way to a glazed door and wooden slat seats. After nearly two years' production both Roe and Brush joined in the building of trolleybus bodywork, the former including a 55-seat lowbridge version for St Helens, and the latter the Mark 2 utility body complete with additional opening windows, upholstered seats and rounded roof domes. Park Royal and Roe followed with these improvements whilst Weymann concentrated on motorbus bodies. Over 320 chassis were built with utility bodywork; amongst the last being two bodied by Park Royal, the final order for new trolleybuses by Pontypridd Urban District Council.

Production of the W continued with bodywork to peacetime specification by the existing builders, together with Northern Coachbuilders and Park Royal. The series included 25 8ft-wide 115hp

15

Top left:
Llanelly & District was a Balfour Beatty subsidiary operating trolleybuses in South Wales. It received five Karrier Ws towards the end of the war. New in 1945, this Roe-bodied bus was sold to Maidstone Corporation in 1952 when the Llanelly system was replaced by South Wales Transport motorbuses. The W in the background was sold to Bradford Corporation and fitted with a new East Lancs body.

Above left:
Lowbridge trolleybuses were always a rarity. Ten Roe-bodied Sunbeam Ws of this layout joined the St Helens Corporation fleet in 1945. The last survived until 1958, the year the system closed.

Centre left:
South Lancashire Transport operated six Weymann-bodied Ws. One is seen here in Bolton in 1951 on the SLT service from Leigh.

Bottom left:
Hastings Tramways, a subsidiary of Maidstone & District from 1935, operated trolleybuses from 1928 to 1957. This is one of 25 Sunbeam Ws for which bodies were supplied by Park Royal, as shown here, and Weymann. This bus saw further service in Bradford.

Above:
Maidstone Corporation received 12 Sunbeams with Northern Coachbuilders bodies in 1946. A semaphore trafficator arm protrudes above the front wheel.

motored versions for Johannesburg of which one had a metal-framed body by Metropolitan-Cammell. The remaining were bodied by Bus Bodies (South Africa).

Production had reached 446 when the model was replaced in 1947 by an updated chassis designated the F4. This was marketed solely under the Sunbeam name and continued in production until the early 1950s with over 300 being built.

OPERATORS RECEIVING NEW KARRIER/SUNBEAM W TROLLEYBUSES

Operator	Quantity
Ashton-under-Lyne	6
Belfast	14
Bradford	37
Darlington	24
Derby	15
Doncaster	9
Grimsby	9
Hastings Tramways	25
Hull	24
Ipswich	22
Llanelly & District	12
Maidstone	17
Mexborough & Swinton	24
Newcastle upon Tyne	18
Nottingham	35
Pontypridd	8
Reading	6
St. Helens	10
South Lancashire Transport	6
South Shields	11
Southend	9
Teesside	8
Walsall	12
Wolverhampton	60
Export	
Johannesburg	25

There is no doubt that the W trolleybus chassis was successful. Many were rebodied, continuing in service on the difficult Bradford system, for

I rode many miles on examples of this model which were quite impressive in performance especially when compared to older, heavier, six-wheeled models with my home system of Nottingham being a typical example.

example, for almost 30 years. The lives of the majority were governed only by decisions to abandon the systems on which they worked. An exception was the six at Reading which, for some unknown reason but possibly coupled to the state of their bodywork, were scrapped after seven years. Many of the Newcastle vehicles saw lives only a little longer.

Looking back

Michael Fowler *looks back 30 years with pictures taken in some of the places he visited in 1962.*

Above:
The fleetname Premier, used by Harold Wilson of Stainforth, lives on in the 1990s with South Yorkshire Transport. In 1962 the company was firmly independent and its coach fleet included this underfloor-engined Guy Arab with stylish Burlingham Seagull body.

Right:
One-man-operated buses were still comparatively rare in 1962, even in rural areas. However Crosville, whose territory encompassed much of rural North Wales, operated over 50 Bristol SC4LKs equipped for OMO. All had 35-seat Eastern Coach Works bodywork. A 1957 example is guided past a parked Morris Minor on the Portmadoc to Morfa Bychan service, while a Ford Prefect waits for the driver to complete his manoeuvre.

Above:
Double-deck Guy Arabs were more usually associated with Premier and were used on services to Doncaster. An Arab III stands alongside an Arab IV, both smartly turned out in Premier's two-tone blue and cream livery.

Left:
Don Motor Services was another Doncaster area independent. The fleet is lined up in 1962; an all-Leyland PD1 bought new, an ex-Maidstone & District Bristol K6A with Weymann body, and a Burlingham-bodied Leyland PD2, also bought new.

Below left:
The Blue Bell fleet of Smith of March included this ex-London Transport AEC Regent III RT. Ex-London RTs were the standard choice for many independent operators at this period.

Above right:
The newest buses in the 17-strong Lowestoft Corporation fleet in 1962 were two Massey-bodied AEC Regent IIIs delivered in 1951. The driver of one waves an Austin Somerset past.

Right:
Fenwick of Old Bolingbroke in Lincolnshire operated this strange coach, a Sentinel with coachwork by Gurney Nutting.

Above left:
Another Lincolnshire operator with a Sentinel – but this time the slightly less unusual bus version – was Simmons of Great Gonerby, who operated under the Reliance name. Simmons' Sentinel is seen at Grantham bus station.

Left:
Yet another rare find was this Daimler CD650, a model which attracted few buyers. With a 150bhp 10.6-litre Daimler engine the CD650 was the most powerful double-decker on sale in Britain and it no doubt seemed a sensible purchase for the hilly terrain around the town when it joined the Halifax Corporation fleet in 1951. The 56-seat body was by East Lancs.

Above:
Two Leyland Tigers PS1s with rear-entrance East Lancs bodies entered service with Preston Corporation in 1949. They were the only single-deckers in the fleet in 1962. They survived untl 1968 and both were subsequently purchased for preservation. Preston's livery at this time was dark maroon and cream.

Centre right:
The 1962 Blackpool Coach Rally attracted sunshine and this sparkling new Bedford VAS with Duple Bella Vista 29-seat body. The Central name lives on in the 1990s in Viscount Central, the coaching arm of Burnley & Pendle Transport.

Right:
These impressive coaches were Leyland Royal Tigers with 41-seat centre-entrance Leyland bodies, still in Alexander's Bluebird livery, although by 1962 in the ownership of Alexander (Fife). They are seen outside Aberdeen railway station.

Above:
Glasgow's last trams ran in 1962. A 1950 Cunarder at Bridgeton Cross is followed by a BUT trolleybus and a Central SMT Leyland Titan.

Below:
Western SMT at Ayr in 1962, with two 1949 Alexander-bodied Leyland Tiger PS1s flanking a 1958 Alexander-bodied Bristol MW6G. The combination of Alexander body and underfloor-engined Bristol chassis was unique to Western. The fleet livery was cream and red.

Bristols in London

Bristol buses have played but a small part in the
capital's transport system. Or have they?
Martin S. Curtis *investigates.*

Passenger vehicles built by the Bristol Tramways
& Carriage Co Ltd or its successors in the bus-
building field, Bristol Commercial Vehicles, were,
until the gradual decline in their numbers
following closure of the Bristol works, to be found
in almost every corner of the United Kingdom,
together with various overseas locations.

In many areas, buses and coaches of Bristol
manufacture dominated the public road transport
scene but one important exception to their
widespread use was London. Rarely have Bristols

been associated with transport in the capital since
this has always been regarded as the domain of
AEC (and to a lesser extent Leyland). Yet, the
numbers of Bristols in London has been

Below:
Among the first Bristols regularly seen in London were B-
type models. Here, Greyhound's B343 (HW 3644) awaits
departure from Prince Street, Bristol to London via
Chippenham and Marlborough – on the country's first
express coach route. B343 was built in 1929 and has
Bristol-built 24-seat coachwork. *M. J. Tozer collection*

Above:
The first Bristols delivered new to London Transport arrived in 1942 and were unfrozen K5Gs with Park Royal austerity bodywork. B5 (FXT 423) displays wartime garb while operating on route 97. *S. L. Poole*

surprisingly high, although their failure to be a main supplier is a reflection of the origins of bus-building in Bristol and London.

Both the London General Omnibus Company and the country's next largest passenger transport operator of the period, Bristol Tramways, were pioneers in the provision of passenger services and greatly influenced early operations. During the late 1900s, both concerns had become dissatisfied with proprietary designs of motor buses and each set about designing and building vehicles to their own specification which led to the establishment of what were later to become two of the nation's leading commercial vehicle builders, while retaining strong links with their respective bus-operating associates.

London General therefore formed AEC whose products, although supplied to many provincial operators, will always be synonymous with the General and later London Transport fleets, while Bristol developed vehicles not only for its own use but also a wide range of other operators. In particular, Bristol became the main chassis supplier to the Tilling group, prior to the formation of the National Bus Company.

Little wonder therefore, that while Bristols were established in strength throughout much of England, Scotland and Wales, they were not seen in great numbers in the Metropolis where the proven AECs had evolved to become the ideal vehicles for the London situation, traditionally operating through much heavier traffic conditions than found elsewhere in the country.

Nevertheless, Bristols managed to penetrate the London barrier following the launch of the highly successful Bristol B-type single-decker which was the first of the company's designs to regularly appear on London's streets, from the 1920s.

The pioneering Greyhound Motors service from Bristol to London, inaugurated in 1925 and regarded as the first long distance express coach service in the country, was operated by Bristol-built vehicles following the takeover of Greyhound Motors by Bristol Tramways in 1928. Other B-types could also be found in London from this period as several operators purchased Bristol buses or coaches, including London & Counties Carriage Co of Croydon, Manor Motor Coaches of Clapham, Thixton & Hoppe and examples even carried General livery for Country Area services, through acquisition of this type with the takeover of Lewis of Watford.

The formation of London Transport in 1933 saw a variety of vehicle types added to the former General fleet, but the predominance of AEC chassis continued and was indeed strengthened as further designs were developed, primarily for London use. Bristol Tramways meanwhile, having joined the Tilling organisation to become its principal chassis supplier, was also improving its range of chassis and was increasingly working with another Tilling concern, Eastern Coach Works of Lowestoft. The reliability and quality of Bristol/ECW products was to become legendary, yet both companies continued to supply customers outside of the Tilling empire and would not necessarily work together – with Bristol's output from its own bodyworks continuing.

As the use of Bristols increased around the country, so did their appearance on express and long distance services to and from London and by the late 1930s they were regularly seen in service with Black & White Motorways, Eastern Counties, Eastern National, United Counties, Western and Southern National (as operators of Royal Blue express services between London and the south-west) and of course Bristol itself on Greyhound services.

In 1939 war came, and the long distance services were interrupted for the duration. Heavy blitz attacks were endured in both London and Bristol with the strain of the conflict spreading across the country. Bus operators were under enormous pressure with bombing raids destroying or badly damaging vehicles while fuel restrictions placed increased demands on public transport, especially where large movements of workers engaged on essential war work was necessary.

Bus manufacturers were required to cease building passenger vehicles and redirect their energies to output directly connected with the war effort, adding further to the pressure on operators as no new vehicles were available. To overcome shortages therefore, buses from fleets which had not suffered quite so severely were loaned to those in most need and a number of further Bristol B-types saw service in London under these circumstances, although the seriousness of the position in Bristol, where the aircraft factories had been subject to direct attack, is reflected by the fact that even London Transport AECs were among those operated on loan to Bristol.

The Government recognised more new buses were required and allowed certain manufacturers to build 'unfrozen' chassis from parts already in stock and in some cases partly assembled. Bristol was among them and the chassis produced were then allocated to operators in greatest need.

London Transport was to benefit from this arrangement and in 1942 received nine Bristol K5G double-deckers powered by Gardner 5LW engines and fitted with austere 56-seat Park Royal bodywork. They operated from Hanwell garage as B1-9 (FXT 419-27) and while welcomed in London, were completely non-standard chassis (as too were the Guy and Daimler double-deckers similarly made available to London Transport).

However, not only were vehicles in short supply but so too was fuel and many road transport operators were encouraged to experiment with gas producers fitted to trailers as a means of consuming less diesel oil and petrol. Among the variety of items produced by Bristol during the war, which included aircraft sections and components, were some 2,500 gas producer trailers, 630 of which were 3T3 and 3T4 types for use with London Transport buses.

Vehicle shortages failed to improve as the war continued but Bristol was permitted to resume bus chassis production, on a limited basis, from 1944. A little more flexibility existed in the allocation and standard of these vehicles and a further 20 K-types were sent to London, although the first of these did not arrive until late 1945. Hostilities had ended by this time of course, but vehicle supply difficulties were to continue for some considerable time.

The new K-types were numbered B10-29 (HGC 235-54) and joined the earlier Bristols at Hanwell. However, these differed in a number of respects to London's earlier K-types since their bodywork, although to utility specification, was built by Duple while power for this batch was provided by AEC 7.7-litre engines (resulting in the designation K6A type) which were rather more familiar to London Transport's engineers. Similar engines later also replaced the Gardner units in the earlier London Ks. In the second batch of Bristols, the engine itself was housed under a much lower bonnet with a new, lower design of PV2-type radiator, which vastly improved driver visibility and remained familiar on new Bristol chassis

Top:
The 1942 K-types were followed by a further 20 in 1945/46, fitted with Duple bodywork and featuring a much lower bonnet and radiator. B11 (HGC 236) mingles among rather more standard London RT buses while working from Hanwell. *S. L. Poole*

Above:
One of the 190 Bristol K-types loaned to London Transport in 1948-50 was Crosville MB325 (JFM 78), a K6A model with lowbridge ECW bodywork. It carries LT names and bull's-eyes on route 118 at Morden station, in July 1949.
Alan B. Cross

until the late 1950s. The London K-types nevertheless remained non-standard and in 1952 the decision was made to withdraw all of London Transport's Bristols, the first moving on to further service with Crosville while the second batch was divided between Brighton Hove & District, Crosville and Lincolnshire in 1953.

In 1948 Bristol Tramways, together with Eastern Coach Works and the Tilling operating companies, were nationalised and in 1955 Bristol's vehicle manufacturing works were separated from the operating company as Bristol Commercial Vehicles Ltd – although remaining under state control. As a result of state ownership, neither Bristol nor ECW could supply customers outside of the nationalised groups, although London Transport was within this category and proposals were put forward for Bristol to design and build a bus which was acceptable to London Transport, in order to take up spare capacity created by the sales restrictions. In fact, Bristol remained fully occupied supplying the state-owned Tilling and Scottish bus groups, together with goods vehicles for British Road Services, while London Transport was anxious to pursue its own vehicle policy with AEC (and Leyland). The Bristol London bus of the 1950s was never to appear therefore – this being a classic example of politicians failing to appreciate that the products of AEC and Bristol, while excellent in their own right, were each tailored to quite different operating circumstances.

Despite this, large numbers of new Bristol double-deckers ran in service with London Transport during 1948-50 as the shortage of new buses remained acute, and no fewer than 190 Bristol/ECW K-types were diverted from Tilling group operators. These represented something of a contrast to the latest LT buses as they featured crash gearboxes rather than the preselective transmission of London's new RT class, and 145 of the Bristols had bodywork of lowbridge

Below:
Although displaying London Transport fleetnames and running numbers, this Bristol J05G with Eastern Counties body also carries Tilling green and cream livery together with Eastern National fleet number 3679. It was among vehicles spending a short time working for LT at Grays when this Christmas 1951 picture was taken.
Alan B. Cross

configuration which involved a far from ideal top deck seating layout – especially for Central London use. Power for these buses was provided by a combination of AEC and Gardner engines.

These Bristols were delivered in their intended operators' liveries which included fleet numbers but lacked fleetnames. Instead they carried London Transport blinds in their destination boxes together with an LT bull's-eye motif on their radiators, and each remained in London for up to 14 months before being released to join their rightful owners: Brighton Hove & District, Caledonian, Crosville, Eastern Counties, Eastern National, Hants & Dorset, Southern National, Southern Vectis, United Auto, United Counties, Westcliff-on-Sea and Western National.

The next group of Bristols to work for London Transport operated in the Grays district between September 1951 and January 1952. This resulted from a reorganisation of routes in this area which involved Eastern National transferring 28 vehicles to the Country Area of London Transport. Included in this arrangement were 11 Bristol J and L type single-deckers which carried LT fleetnames and running-numbers on their Tilling green and cream paintwork until 2 January 1952, when the Bristols were sold back to Eastern National and standard London Transport buses took over the Grays services.

During the following year, London Transport was seeking operational experience of lightweight, underfloor-engined single-deckers and while the recently introduced RF class AEC Regal IV remained LT's standard saloon, comparative trials were conducted between a Leyland Tiger Cub, an AEC Monocoach, and a Bristol/ECW LS5G belonging to Bristol Tramways' own fleet, number

1950s and 1960s. In most cases rolling stock took the form of Bristol's underfloor-engined LS or MW models with full coach, express or dual purpose bodywork, although exceptions regularly seen at London's Victoria Coach Station included Eastern Counties' Bristol SC forward-engined single-deckers and Western/Southern National's small underfloor-engined SUL coaches. A succession of Bristol double-deckers also regularly appeared in London on services provided by Thames Valley from the west and Eastern National from the east.

In 1963, Bristol's highly successful, rear-engined RELH made its debut on front line express work into London, initially with ECW coachwork and later still underfloor-engined LH coaches were also seen on some routes.

Having already been released from sales restrictions, Bristol Commercial Vehicles' ownership was shared equally between British Leyland and the newly formed National Bus Company from 1969. This further increased the

2828 (PHW 918). The LS was delivered new to Bristol in full London Transport Green Line livery and caused something of a stir when it entered service in this condition from Bath. It was then loaned to LT for a year from April 1953 and operated from Reigate on both Country Area bus and Green Line coach routes, together with Central Area services from Dalston. During this period, its five-speed synchromesh gearbox was replaced with Hobbs semi-automatic transmission.

No LS orders followed, and it was to be 21 years before London Transport next operated Bristol-built vehicles – by which time both Bristol and ECW were trading freely again, following Leyland Motors having taken a stake in the companies from 1965. Meanwhile, the number of operators using Bristols to provide services into London from almost every part of the country had increased, with services of the Tilling group being operated by Bristols almost exclusively during the

Above:
Hurrying along Buckingham Palace Road is Western SMT KT2347, a 12m long Alexander-bodied REMH motorway coach used almost exclusively on services between Glasgow and London. *M. S. Curtis*

degree to which Bristols were used on coach services and RE coaches in particular, usually with ECW or Plaxton coachwork, became increasingly familiar on NBC's subsidiaries' express services - which formed the basis of the National Express network with vehicles appearing in all-white livery from the early 1970s.

NBC's London-based coaching units, Tillings Transport and Timpsons were among the Bristol operators, but perhaps the most spectacular Bristol coaches to be seen in London were the amazing ECW-bodied VRL/LH double-deckers. Thirty such vehicles worked on Standerwick express routes between London and the North-west but were unfortunately withdrawn prematurely following a series of mechanical difficulties and a tragic accident involving one of these coaches overturning on the M1 motorway when its driver attempted to swerve to avoid the debris of an earlier collision. Upon their withdrawal however, no fewer than 16 VRLs moved directly into London for sightseeing work with Destination London, International Coach Lines and Thomas Cook. Some actually worked on hire to LT for its Round London Sightseeing Tour as did Bristol VRT double-deckers of Alder Valley (the successor to Thames Valley) between the peak periods when not required for longer distance commuter services.

Below:
London Transport's BL class comprised 95 7ft 6in wide Bristol LH6Ls with ECW 39-seat bodywork, such as BL7, on the 250 at Romford. *M. S. Curtis*

While the National Bus Company covered England and Wales, Bristols operated for the Scottish Bus Group too, with convoys of Alexander-bodied RE coaches, including the REMH models of Scottish Omnibuses and Western SMT, working the overnight services from London to Edinburgh and Glasgow.

Bristol chassis also found favour with independent companies at this time, with Grey Green and Margo being among the largest based in London to run LH coaches. The number of Bristols in central London during the early and mid-1970s was therefore greater than at any other time.

London Transport's next encounter with Bristols came in 1975. By this time AEC was no longer in a position to meet LT's requirements and for several years off-the-peg buses, rather than those to its own design, had been less than entirely successful in London conditions. In some cases Ford Transit minibuses had been introduced but when these services needed upgrading, London Transport rather surprisingly bought the first of 17 Bristol/ECW LHS types (numbered BS1-17) with manual transmission (which itself was rare on full-size London buses), Leyland 401 engine and an ultra-short 26-seat body with the minimum rear overhang - to a design not seen before. At only 24ft long, this was over 2ft shorter than was usual for an ECW-bodied LHS, and would have given the London vehicles a unique appearance had similar vehicles not been produced simultaneously for West Yorkshire PTE.

Replacement of London's AEC RF class saloons was also due and since LT particularly wanted 7ft 6in-wide vehicles it was decided that longer ECW-bodied LHs would be suitable, and the forerunner of the BL class of 95 such vehicles was constructed in 1975, with deliveries following until 1977.

These differed from the BS types in a number of respects and reflected a degree of London influence in their design. They were based on standard LH6L chassis with 30ft long 39-seat bodies and also featured semi-automatic transmission, power steering, and slightly modified cab and entrance step arrangements. The final three of these vehicles were operated in conjunction with Hillingdon Borough Council.

While LHs were introduced into inner London, the country services were moving even further away from London Transport traditions as these had been separated from the main LT fleet in 1970 to form London Country Bus Services – an NBC subsidiary. As such, it too naturally looked to Bristol to supply some of its new vehicles when fleet replacement was under consideration and

once again the LH model was chosen. Unlike most of those in the red London fleet however, all of the green country versions were LHS models with manual transmissions. These carried 35-seat standard length (26ft) ECW bodywork – the first 23 of which (also known as BL class) were built to 8ft width while the following 44 carried 7ft 6in-wide bodies and were classified BN. The last of these were delivered in 1977.

During this period, London Country operated two other Bristol models as several MW coaches

Provincial Bristols, mainly in the ownership of NBC companies, continued to maintain services into London from throughout the country although the use of REs waned as the emphasis on Bristol production moved significantly away from this model to concentrate rather more on double-deck chassis. Some of the traditional users of Bristols on express services therefore defected to other manufacturers' models.

From 1979, a new double-deck model was introduced by Bristol, known initially as the B45-type but later as the Leyland Olympian, and this replaced the VRT from 1981. Despite NBC's half ownership of Bristol, the curious use of the Leyland name on this and several less well known Bristol chassis seemed extraordinary – although new Olympians were usually licensed as Bristols at this time.

In London, long-wheelbase Olympians appeared on services operated by Alder Valley, Maidstone & District and Wessex carrying ECW double-deck coach bodies, while shorter versions ran with London Country with Roe bus bodywork. These however were to be among the last new 'Bristols' to work in London, for the Bristol works were to close in September 1983 following NBC's disposal of its interest in the business the previous year.

Olympian production was transferred north where it really did become a Leyland, while the number of Bristols regularly seen in the capital has now begun to decline – but not completely eliminated as several have been given a new lease of life working with independents (including on LRT tendered routes), some 70 years after the arrival of the earliest Bristols in London.

were hired from Western National while a batch of 15 new VRT double deckers was bought in 1977 with highbridge 74-seat bodywork and Leyland 501 engines, although most London Country rear-engined double-deckers at the time were Leyland Atlanteans. These buses (numbered BT1-15) operated from Grays but were completely non-standard so when a requirement for additional double-deckers arose with Bristol Omnibus (as Bristol Tramways had become), the entire batch was transferred to Bristol in the early 1980s.

Bristols owned by London Transport and London Country

London Transport

Fleet nos	Registration nos	Chassis type	Body make	Seats	Date new
B1-9*	FXT419-427	K5G	Park Royal	H56R	1942
B10-29	HGC235-254	K6A	Duple	H56R	1945/46
BL1-40	KJD401-440P	LH6L	ECW	B39F	1976
BL41-95	OJD41-95R	LH6L	ECW	B39F	1976/77
BS1-6	GHV501-506N	LHS6L	ECW	B26F	1975
BS7-17	OJD7-17R	LHS6L	ECW	B26F	1976

B1-9 were originally allocated fleet numbers STB1-9

London Country

Fleet nos	Registration nos	Chassis type	Body make	Seats	Date new
BL1-11	RPH101-111L	LHS6L	ECW	B35F	1973
BL12-23	SPK112-123M	LHS6L	ECW	B35F	1973
BN24-30	XPD124-130N	LHS6L	ECW	B35F	1974
BN31-53	GPD299-321N	LHS6L	ECW	B35F	1974
BN54-67	TPJ54-67S	LHS6L	ECW	B35F	1977
BT1-15	PPH461-475R	VRT/SL3	ECW	H74F	1977

Above:
Regular operation of Bristol LHs by London Buses ceased in 1990 and one of the last routes was the C11 which served King's Cross. This is a 1983 view when London's single-deck livery was unrelieved red. *Stewart J. Brown*

Below:
Most of the Bristols serving London have been those on express services. A 1970 RELH of Bristol Omnibus at Victoria in 1973 illustrates the point. It has a 49-seat Eastern Coach Works body. *Stewart J. Brown*

Chaos out of order?

The British bus business is in a state of flux,
Stewart J. Brown *looks at some of the changes of the last 20 years.*

The 1972/73 edition of Ian Allan's *Little Red Book* is a revealing document. I've blown 20 years of dust and cobwebs off it (to discover it cost only £3.30 all these years ago) and it's open on my desk now at a page which includes Gelligaer Urban District Council Omnibus Department with 26 buses under the charge of an Omnibus Manager. The next entry is Glasgow Corporation Transport with 1,225 buses. On the facing page is Merthyr Tydfil Corporation Omnibus Department with 79 buses.

I flick back a few dusty pages, to the London Transport Executive. LTE had 5,976 'oil-engined vehicles of AEC, Leyland and Daimler manufacture'. The quaint description 'oil-engined' seems pedantic for 1972, even for LTE. Did they think we'd imagine they were still running petrol-engined buses?

I flick forward to the National Bus Company section. As the dust settles I spy Greenslades Tours of Exeter: 112 coaches. Is it a misprint? Surely Greenslades was never that big. Don't they mean 12? Ribble Motor Services had 1,019 buses and coaches; Southdown, 750. The Scottish Bus Group had seven subsidiaries. The biggest was Western SMT with 981 buses.

The index to advertisers includes the Arlington Motor Co: 'over 50 years' service to the PSV industry'. It had a few more years service to give, only ceasing to serve in 1989. Then there are Duple Coachbuilders, Ford Motor Co, Marshall of Cambridge, Metro-Cammell Weymann and even

Below:
Gelligaer's fleet of omnibuses on the eve of its absorption by Rhymney Valley District Council. A Northern Counties-bodied Bristol VRT leads an assortment of single-deckers.

Strachans (Coachbuilders) who were about 15 years ahead of their time with an advert for a 16-seat Pacemaker body on a Ford Transit chassis. Heart surgery was still in its infancy; the Strachans' Pacemaker wasn't designed to make anyone's heart beat faster.

I reach over for the 1990 edition; there's no dust on this one, it's the one which usually sits on my desk. Gelligaer, Glasgow and Merthyr Tydfil have gone – well, at least their municipal buses have gone. The towns are still there, although what's left of my beloved Glasgow has survived despite the best efforts of the city's planners rather than because of them.

Merthyr Tydfil Transport's buses vanished abruptly and without trace in 1989. Gelligaer's were a victim first of local government reorganisation in 1974, which saw them absorbed

Above:
Ribble had over 1,000 buses in 1972, including lowbridge Leyland Atlanteans. One approaches Blackburn later in the decade.

by Rhymney Valley District Council, and then of National Welsh rapacity in 1989 which brought an end to the RVDC fleet – as it did to MTT.

The spiritual successor to Glasgow Corporation Transport is Strathclyde Buses – still referred to by many of its older users as 'the Corporation', despite changes of livery, changes of ownership, changes of management, deregulation, and expensive marketing campaigns. In all of which there must be a lesson – perhaps the one that led newly-privatised Eastern Scottish to revert in 1990 to the fleetname SMT, abandoned quarter of a century earlier but still part of the lingua franca of the stolid citizenry of Scotland's stolid capital.

Strathclyde's fleet in the 1990 *Little Red Book* is 773 buses – and it has a larger operating area than GCT had 20 years earlier. Of the 773, only 657 are double-deckers. There were 1,209 Corporation double-deckers plying Glasgow's streets in 1972. How did they fit them all in?

Not that Glaswegians are being deprived of buses. Far from it. But even the Scottish Bus Group subsidiaries who have moved in to compete with Strathclyde Buses have shrunk in size. Kelvin Central Buses is an uncomfortable amalgam of what in 1972 was Central SMT with

Left:
London Transport's fleet was just under the 6,000 mark in 1972 and still included venerable types such as this RT-class AEC Regent entering Trafalgar Square.

Top:
Change in the 1970s. A 1966 Leyland Titan PD3 of
Southdown in the company's traditional livery. The
corporate National Bus Company advertisements give a
hint of the changes taking place. *Stewart J. Brown*

Above:
Merthyr Tydfil's standard bus — the East Lancs-bodied
Leyland Leopard. This is a 1965 L1, photographed in 1974.
Stewart J. Brown

bits of Scottish Omnibuses and Alexander (Midland). KCB had 569 buses when the 1990 *Little Red Book* was compiled. Central SMT alone had more – 613 – in 1972. Western, incidentally, remained the group's biggest subsidiary with 796 buses in 1990, although in the intervening years its northern area had been parcelled off and reformed as Clydeside, only for the whole operation to be reunited after a disastrous financial performance by Clydeside in the highly competitive Glasgow area.

The differences – and similarities – between Central and Kelvin Central are interesting. Despite growing interest in decidedly unsuitable

high-floor Leyland Leopards for its predominantly urban operations, the Central fleet still included 463 double-deckers in 1972, mostly Bristol Lodekkas.

The fleet livery was red and cream, little changed for decades. Its operating area was industrial Lanarkshire and that part of Dunbartonshire which hugs the north bank of the Clyde – running out as far as Helensburgh. Here it connected with Garelochhead Coach Services (39 buses, including 10 double-deckers, mostly bought new) but now no more.

Before its amalgamation with Central in 1989, Kelvin in its brief but exciting four-year life had

Above left:
Orderly days in Glasgow. This Leyland Titan PD2 with Alexander body built using Weymann parts was delivered in 1955 and operated until 1969 when it was replaced by a Leyland Atlantean.

Left:
When this Atlantean was delivered to the Greater Glasgow PTE in 1980, new AN68 models were displacing ageing PDR1s from the fleet.

Above:
An East Lancs-bodied Leyland Leopard in the Merthyr Tydfil fleet alongside its replacement, a Leyland Lynx. The Lynxes, in a bright new livery, ushered in a new but short-lived era in the town.

Right:
The South Yorkshire PTE swallowed up most of the Doncaster area independents. A 1971 Daimler Fleetline with 78-seat Roe body, taken over with the Felix Motors business in 1976, stands in central Doncaster.

three distinctly different liveries and a varied fleet. The combined KCB fleet in 1990 still contained high-floor Leopards...

Central, in its death throes at the start of 1989, clutched as a drowning man at the straws of long-past glory and revived a blue and grey livery for its Airdrie services (after Baxter's Bus Service, taken over by SBG in 1962) and a green and cream livery for East Kilbride (after Chieftain, taken over in 1961). Did any passengers at the end of the 1980s really remember Baxter and Chieftain?

These identities were short-lived but a third new livery, red and cream, was adopted as standard in late 1990 and applied to blue Kelvin buses, dark

red Central buses, green Chieftain buses and the blue and grey Monklands Buses in Airdrie.

Chaotic, but colourful – especially if you add the yellow fronts applied crudely to some of the liveries after Kelvin and Central were combined at the start of the year.

LTE has gone. Between 1972 and 1990 what is now London Buses had lost 1,000 vehicles with its fleet down from 5,976 to 4,915. But who would have forecast in 1972 that its 1990 fleet would still include some of the AEC Routemasters then in service, rubbing shoulders with such alien marques as DAF, Mercedes-Benz, Renault, Scania and Volvo. Some of the 1,000 missing buses can

Above:
Glasgow Corporation in 1973 with an Alexander-bodied Daimler CVG6 in St Enoch Square — still a terminal 20 years later, although much altered. *Stewart J. Brown*

Below:
Two-door buses and one-man-operation still had some novelty value in the early 1970s, when Glasgow Corporation enjoyed a monopoly of bus services within the city boundary. Castlemilk, the destination of this Atlantean, was to become an area of competitive activity after deregulation in 1986. *Stewart J. Brown*

Right:
Despite changes of livery and ownership the Corporation name lived on amongst users of Glasgow's buses. The first PTE livery on an Alexander-bodied Ailsa in 1976. *Stewart J. Brown*

be attributed to the success of private sector operators in winning tenders from London Transport. To add insult to injury some even used ex-London buses, but that was in the early days. As tendering developed more and more operators – including London Buses – quoted on the basis of supplying new vehicles despite the very shaky tenure which a three-year contract gave them.

NBC has gone but there's still a company called Greenslades Tours with 53 vehicles, although it's not a direct successor to the erstwhile British Electric Traction group company. Ribble is still around but at half its previous size (541 vehicles), as is Southdown, listed as owning only 208 vehicles in 1990.

I imagined that part of the explanation for the contraction of Southdown lay in the expansion of

what was the Brighton Hove & District Omnibus Company. But a quick look at the 1972/73 *Little Red Book* shows that BH&D had only 153 buses. In 1990 the Brighton & Hove Bus & Coach Co, successor to BH&D, has 189 vehicles, Southdown, where are you now?

A subsidiary of Stagecoach is the answer, although the company in fact expanded under Stagecoach control with the absorption of Portsmouth CityBus.

You'll look in vain for Stagecoach in a 1970s edition of the *Little Red Book*. Stagecoach was a child of the 1980 Transport Act which deregulated express coach services. The whole idea of regulating what is essentially a leisure market seems strange now, but licences to run express coaches were fiercely contested and established operating groups (plus British Rail) united in traffic court battles to keep out would-be newcomers.

Stagecoach started running express services in Scotland in 1980 and soon expanded into Anglo-

Above:
Old-established London coach operator Grey Green now runs more buses than coaches. Its most prestigious tendered route is the 24, which takes it through the heart of London. The service is operated by Alexander-bodied Volvo Citybuses.

Below:
And who would have forecast the presence of foreign vehicles in the London Buses heartland in the 1990s? In 1989 Scania – foreign to the extent of not even being manufactured in the EEC – supplied double-deckers and a solitary Alexander-bodied single-decker.

Above:
The order of the Scottish Bus Group was reduced to chaos in the 1980s. An Alexander-bodied Leyland Titan PD3A of Western SMT in Glasgow in 1977 gives an impression of solidity and continuity which was soon to vanish.
Stewart J. Brown

Left:
Kelvin Scottish was a short-lived Scottish Bus Group operation to the north of the Clyde. This Daimler Fleetline had previously been operated by Alexander (Midland). It is seen in Glasgow in 1987.   *Stewart J. Brown*

Below left:
A victim of the chaos: Graham's Bus Service of Paisley vanished without trace in 1991. A Fleetline, purchased new, passes Paisley Cross in happier days.   *Stewart J. Brown*

Above right:
In 1977, when this venerable RT-type AEC Regent was nearing the end of its days, it seemed inconceivable that London could ever be served by buses which were anything but red. This is Trafalgar Square, where 15 years later the buses of two private operators can also be seen in regular service.   *Stewart J. Brown*

Right:
Grey Green moved from being a coach operator to a bus operator as a result of winning tendered services in London. A former South Yorkshire Metrobus awaits customers in Enfield in 1988 in the company's original and short-lived bus livery.   *Stewart J. Brown*

Scottish services, much to the chagrin of the Scottish Bus Group 'which thought its position unassailable. Stagecoach – and other less successful operators – invested in new high-specification coaches and ultimately goaded SBG to action in the form of Scottish Citylink, a high-

profile re-branding of the disparate collection of services run by its subsidiaries.

Now Stagecoach owns Ribble, East Midland, Southdown, Cumberland, United Counties, Hampshire Bus and Hastings & District. Not to mention Magicbus, Inverness Traction and Northern Scottish in Scotland.

The 1990 *Little Red Book* advertisers index includes only one name that was there in 1972/73; Norbury, manufacturers of destination blinds for the bus operating gentry.

The point of all this? What links Merthyr Tydfil and Glasgow and Kelvin Central and Stagecoach and London Transport? Change, change and more change.

Who would have believed that Merthyr Tydfil could vanish without trace? Or that Southdown could shrink so dramatically?

The pace of change in Britain's bus and coach industry since deregulation and the start of privatisation in 1986 has been remarkable. It has been the period of most rapid change since the the late 1920s and early 1930s when vehicle design was progressing rapidly, companies were growing and new big bus groups were emerging.

Vehicle design continues to progress (more rapidly elsewhere in Europe than in Britain) and new big bus groups continue to emerge. But the industry is in decline as fleet sizes overall continue to shrink.

There has always been change. Remember the Paisley independents? There were four in 1972; Cunningham (14 vehicles), Graham (23), McGill (19) and Paton (33). Only McGill – now with 18 Leyland Nationals – survives. Similarly there were

the colourful Doncaster independents – Blue Ensign Coaches, Felix Motors, Leon Motor Services, Samuel Morgan (Blue Line), Rossie Motors (Rossington), T Severn & Sons, R Store (Reliance Motors) and Harold Wilson (Premier). This litany of colourful operators owned over 50 double-decker buses, not to mention single-deckers and coaches. Most were swallowed up by the South Yorkshire Passenger Transport Executive in the 1970s as it pursued a ruthless policy of co-ordination by acquisition.

The creation of the National Bus Company in 1969 saw massive changes as ex-Tilling and ex-BET group companies were united and – horror of horrors – a corporate livery is bearable if it's attractive and well executed. Few are.

So change is nothing new. But don't you ever hanker after just a little bit less change? I don't mind chaos as long as there's some order to it.

Which there was once. When Glasgow Corporation was running its 1,225 buses there was a nice steady programme of fleet replacement. In would come Alexander-bodied Leyland Atlanteans, as they had done since 1962 and as they would do until 1981. Out went older buses. The first Atlanteans replaced the final trams, later Atlanteans replaced the city's trolleybuses (some of which were only nine years old), and then it was on to a simple cycle. In came a new Atlantean, out went an old Daimler CVG6 or Leyland Titan PD2 or AEC Regent. Nice and orderly.

Even at Merthyr Tydfil there was order. Its 79 buses in 1972/73 were all East Lancs-bodied

Above:
Prophetic? Or just ironic? Two Southdown Bristol VRTs carry Stagecoach branding for a coastal limited-stop service in 1985.

Leylands. The older ones were Titans, the newer ones Leopards. Double-deck operations were being phased out as single-deckers, mostly Leopards, replaced the Titans. Merthyr Tydfil did have occasional outbreaks of excitement: Bristol REs and Metro-Scanias, for example. It switched to Leyland Lynxes in what should have been its

Below:
The Bee Line Buzz Company was launched by United Transport in 1987 with a fleet of new minibuses and the express aim of raising standards. Northern Counties-bodied 50 Dodge S46s for the operation.

All change in Manchester. On the right a Ribble Leyland Olympian in Stagecoach livery. On the left a Mercedes Benz of the Bee Line Buzz Company, owned by Drawlane, when photographed in the summer of 1990.
Stewart J. Brown

finest but turned out to be its final hour, and the Lynxes replaced Leopards which had replaced Titans. Order is everything.

As I write the MTT depot still stands in Nantygwenith Street, abandoned. It is lettered Merthyr Tydfil Transport Ltd – the addition of 'Ltd' bearing witness to the new commercialism which ultimately killed the operation.

Much of the blame for Merthyr Tydfil's troubles (and those of nearby Rhymney Valley and Taff Ely) can be laid at the door of National Welsh, which entered into the spirit of competition rather more wholeheartedly than most other bus operators. However, National Welsh got its come-uppance in 1990 as it ran into financial problems and had to make severe cutbacks, before selling its eastern operations to Western Travel as Red & White. But that was a bit too late for Merthyr Tydfil.

What change there was in the 1970s was generally to do with the disappearance of operators. NBC amalgamated some of its neighbouring subsidiaries in the 1970s, only to split them up in to smaller and more manageable units in the 1980s. Indeed National Welsh was an NBC creation. Look in the 1972/73 *Little Red Book* under the NBC heading and you'll find Jones Omnibus Services and Red & White Services and Western Welsh – but no National Welsh.

Now there is a slowly emerging new order. NBC has gone as if it had never existed. The odd preserved bus in the much-maligned corporate poppy red or leaf green serving as the only tangible reminder of what was at its peak the world's biggest bus company. SBG is following it. New groups are growing. Badgerline, Caldaire, Stagecoach and Drawlane, to name but the biggest.

One of Drawlane's subsidiaries is the Bee Line Buzz Co in Manchester. Bee Line illustrates in microcosm both the positive and negative aspects of change. Conceived by United Transport – and whatever happened to them, you might well ask – as a friendly customer-oriented minibus service with smart modern vehicles, Bee Line started operating in Manchester in April 1987. Ribble bought it in September 1988. Ribble was bought by Stagecoach in April 1989 and in September Stagecoach sold the Bee Line operation to Drawlane, along with some of the Stagecoach group's other interests in the Manchester area. Drawlane quickly turned the Bee Line into the antithesis of all United had planned, with a fleet of dowdy old double-deckers, many running in the liveries of their previous owners.

Riches to rags. Order to chaos.

Below:
By 1989 the Bee Line operation had been owned by Ribble, then Stagecoach and finally Drawlane and vehicle standards had been lowered to the point where it was running 17-year-old double-deckers in their previous owners' liveries. Still carrying Ribble fleetnames a former Greater Manchester Transport Atlantean has had yellow paint applied to the lower front panel of its Park Royal body to identify it as a Bee Line bus.

Vanishing body-builders

Britain's bus body-building industry has experienced tremendous upheaval, **Alan Millar** *considers the changes and their causes.*

Forty years ago, one of Britain's most successful double-deck bus designs was launched. It was exactly what the market wanted then, it became a familiar sight on town and city streets from

Below:
Birmingham Corporation was a major Metro-Cammell customer in the 1950s and 1960s. A 1951 Daimler CVD6 passes a 1964 Fleetline. *A. D. Broughall*

Aberdeen to Plymouth, Maidstone to Derry, and remained in production for 16 years.

Two years ago, its manufacturer went out of business, a victim of a declining market and its own failure to survive the immense change which has swept through the industry.

The manufacturer was Metro-Cammell Weymann, the rip-roaring success was its Orion lightweight body of 1952 and its subsequent fate

Top:
The standard BET-style single-deck bus body was produced by a number of builders. Marshall was responsible for the body on this Ribble Leyland Leopard PSU3, looking slightly battle-scarred in this 1974 view in Blackburn bus station. *Stewart J. Brown*

Above:
The basic BET shell was capable of some variation. This Marshall-bodied AEC Reliance of South Wales Transport has short bays, cream window rubbers, polished beading and 41 dual-purpose seats. *Stewart J. Brown*

Right:
Alexander has produced a series of stylish double- and single-deck bodies over the last 30 years, and found new customers too! But this did not stop the company changing hands and cutting its size in 1990. Edinburgh has been a traditional buyer of Alexander bodywork. This is a PDR1A Atlantean. *Stewart J. Brown*

Above:
A Leyland Tiger Cub demonstrator was built with MCW's Hermes body. It later joined the Merthyr Tydfil fleet.
Alan Millar

Below:
MCW helped Leyland with early rear-engined double-deck developments. One of the Leyland low-loader prototypes had what was in effect a low-height Orion body.
Stewart J. Brown

helps explain just how dramatically the bodybuilding industry has changed in that period.

Compared with chassis manufacturing, bodybuilding has fared relatively well. We are still virtually self-sufficient in bus bodywork and build about half of our coach bodies. By 1990, six major British bodybuilders survived in the market – Alexander, Plaxton, Leyland, East Lancs, Northern Counties and Optare. All are part of larger

concerns and none was a market leader even 25 years ago.

They have survived partly because bodybuilding lends itself to smaller scale companies close to the customer. The body is a relatively low technology product, it takes up more space than a chassis, is slower to build, less easy to transport over long distances and is part of the bus or coach most likely to be customised to meet the needs of a local market.

Our most peculiar requirements, double-deckers and right-hand drive, have helped deter Continental bodybuilders from attacking the British bus market. So has our reluctance to pay for the more expensive products built for European cities.

British bus bodying was revolutionised in the 1930s when leading manufacturers began to phase out composite construction, using timber framing, and moved to longer-lasting metal framing. MCW was a product of that time, bringing together the bus bodying activities of train builder Metro-Cammell of Birmingham and Weymann of Addlestone, Surrey. It began life at the head office of the Vickers group, but later became part of the Laird shipbuilding and engineering group.

By 1949, its principal competitors were owned by Associated Commercial Vehicles, AEC's parent company. ACV had got into bodybuilding the previous year when it bought Crossley, whose bodywork sold more widely than its bus chassis, notably to several of the big cities. It consolidated its position in 1949 when it bought West London-based Park Royal Vehicles and its Leeds subsidiary, Charles H. Roe, which continued to build composite bodies, mainly but by no means exclusively for operators in the North of England. The three bodybuilders' sales organisations were combined in 1955.

Leyland built its own range of all-metal bus and coach bodies exclusively on its own chassis.

The fortunes of two other manufacturers were tied closely to big operating groups. Alexander had begun life as the Scottish Motor Traction group's in-house bodybuilder, but escaped nationalisation in 1949 and began to develop a wider customer base. Eastern Coach Works was the in-house builder for the Tilling group, but its Lowestoft works joined Bristol Commercial Vehicles in state ownership when the Tilling companies were nationalised in 1948 and was kept off the open market for the next 17 years.

Northern Counties and East Lancs had loyal customers, mainly among small-to-medium sized North of England operators.

The wood-framed coach market was dominated by Hendon, North London-based Duple which,

Above:
MCW was a key supplier of double-deck bodies on Leyland Atlantean chassis to the BET group. Among its customers was Maidstone & District. A lowheight PDR1 picks up passengers in Eastbourne. *Alan Millar*

thanks to a marketing arrangement with Bedford, was the only bodybuilder which could claim national coverage. Its Vista-bodied Bedford OBs were very much the standard coach of the late 1940s. Its closest rivals were Blackpool-based Burlingham which, like Duple, also built buses and Harrington, based in Hove. Plaxton's Scarborough-built products then had a much more regional following.

Many smaller bodybuilders withdrew from the bus and coach market in the early 1950s, as demand fell and larger operators were prepared to wait for standard products from larger suppliers. Saunders-Roe and Scottish Aviation reverted to the defence business, Brush and Cravens to railway manufacturing, Charles Roberts to truck bodies.

MCW, Park Royal and Leyland all benefited from London Transport's huge postwar re-equipment programme which also called for bodies completed to precise measurements so they could be swapped from chassis to chassis during overhaul at LT's new Aldenham works.

Between 1947 and 1954, LT bought 6,806 AEC and Leyland RT-type double-deckers. Park Royal supplied 48%, MCW 37%, Leyland 7%, with the balance coming from two smaller suppliers, Saunders and Cravens, the 120 Cravens bodies being the only ones which did not conform to the standard design. Metro-Cammell supplied all 700 bodies for the RF class of underfloor-engined AEC Regal IVs delivered in 1951-53.

Over the same period, Birmingham Corporation was replacing its trams and bought over 1,600

Left:
Van Hool-McArdle made little impression on the British bus market. The only fleet order came from South Yorkshire, for bodies on Ailsas. *Stewart J. Brown*

Above:
With its roots going back in the mists of time who would have forecast the demise of Metro-Cammell Weymann? This four-bay Orion style body was built by Weymann for Swindon Corporation in 1962. Weymann was to close a few years later. *Stewart J. Brown*

Below:
MCW moved into co-operative ventures with Scania, one of which was the Metropolitan double-decker. The Tyne & Wear PTE was a major user of the type. *Stewart J. Brown*

double-deckers, 970 bodied by MCW, 490 by
Crossley. MCW had similar success in Manchester
which bought nearly 900 double-deckers, 435
from MCW and 270 from Crossley. The same sort
of story was being repeated around the country.

Leyland beat AEC in the race to develop integral
construction – chassisless – buses and had its
underfloor-engined Olympic single-decker
available in 1949. But rather than body it in its
own still busy works, it developed the bus jointly
with MCW and five years later pulled out of bus
bodying altogether.

The Olympic enjoyed limited home market
success, but remained in production for export
until 1970. It went on to spawn the Royal Tiger
chassis in 1950 and, as the industry became
weight conscious, the Tiger Cub in 1953. A
Leyland/MCW integral version of the Tiger Cub,
the Olympian, had brief success, but the
Olympic's real significance for MCW was in
bringing it closer to Leyland and making it many
British and overseas operators' first choice of
bodybuilder when buying Leyland or other
chassis.

MCW supplied large numbers of its Hermes
bodies on Tiger Cub chassis, notably to some of
the British Electric Traction group companies in
England and Wales and it was to do even better
with its new double-deck design.

Up till the 1950s, Metro-Cammell and Weymann
had their own separate identities and, with
notable exceptions like the London RTs, rarely
built each others' designs. The Hermes started to
change that and in 1952 the prototype Orion
lightweight double-decker was shown on a
Daimler chassis for PMT. This was a child of the
new frugal age, with glass fibre front and rear roof
domes and much bare metal where traditionally
polished wood had gone before.

It may have lacked the craftsmanship of its
predecessors, but at just over six tons, the
prototype was a full two tons lighter than the
typical double-decker of its day. Fuel savings of
two miles per gallon were reckoned to be possible
in some cases.

The Orion was a standard, but adaptable
design. Available in highbridge, lowbridge and
lowheight form, with forward or rear entrance (in
Bournemouth's case with both), with full front or
half cab, four or five-bay construction. It adapted
easily to the new 30ft length which was permitted
from 1956 and was fitted on Leyland, AEC,
Daimler, Dennis and Guy chassis.

Weymann offered its own body design as an
alternative to the Orion for a time, but the Orion
was the undoubted success story of the 1950s
and into the 1960s. The customer list was
impressive. City fleets in Manchester, Salford,

Above:
**Best-seller, 1950s style. A Metro-Cammell Orion body in
the Aberdeen Corporation fleet. It is on a Daimler CVG6
chassis.** *Stewart J. Brown*

Liverpool, Edinburgh, Aberdeen, Dundee,
Sheffield, Leeds, Coventry, Wolverhampton and
Plymouth alone took over 1,700. BET companies
Ribble, Northern General, Trent, East Midland,
PMT, South Wales, Western Welsh, Rhondda and
Maidstone & District took over 700.

There were many more orders: Bradford,
Halifax, Bolton, Newcastle, Portsmouth, Brighton,
Nottingham, Lancashire United, Hebble, Yorkshire
Woollen, Aldershot & District – the list went on.
And there was more to come.

With its own bodyworks closing, Leyland turned
to MCW to help it develop the Atlantean, Britain's
first rear-engined double-decker. One of its 1954
prototype rear-entrance/rear-engined Lowloader
double-decks had a lowheight Orion-style body
and two years later the first Atlantean appeared
as a lowheight integral with a body which owed
much to the Orion design.

When Atlantean production began two years
later, it was a simpler vehicle with a separate
chassis, but MCW took the lion's share of early
orders with highbridge and lowbridge bodies
clearly developed from the Orion. It was well

placed to body the rival Daimler Fleetline when it appeared in 1960.

Between 1958 and 1963, over 370 of these bodies were supplied to three BET companies, Maidstone & District, Ribble and Western Welsh, and as Birmingham, Manchester and Newcastle started buying rear-engined buses in quantity, the Orion derivative figured highly in their orders.

ACV's integral single-decker, the Monocoach, was launched with the AEC Reliance in 1953. Most were bodied by Park Royal, but it died an early death and ACV did better with integral double-deckers.

Park Royal and AEC worked closely with London Transport to develop the integral aluminium-bodied Routemaster, the next and final development of the traditional front-engined London bus, which appeared in prototype form in 1954.

They had competitors, a Leyland/MCW Routemaster built by Weymann and a Leyland/ECW prototype, but ACV priced the job cleverly enough to ensure that the entire production run of over 2,800 was built by Park Royal between 1958 and 1967.

The Routemaster led in 1956 to the Bridgemaster, ACV's answer to the nationalised operators' Bristol/ECW Lodekka of 1949, the first lowheight double-decker with highbridge seating layout on both decks.

Crossley developed this bus which combined the Routemaster's suspension system and aluminium integral construction with a synchromesh gearbox and air brakes which were more acceptable to provincial operators. Production was soon moved to Park Royal and the body specification was changed to meet the BET group's requirement for steel framing and styling which owed a passing influence to the MCW Orion. Only 179 Bridgemasters were built before it gave way to the separate-chassised Renown in 1963.

Crossley was closed in 1958 and ACV developed a wider role for Roe, building steel-framed bodies for BET and other customers, notably on Atlanteans for Northern General, Devon General and Kingston upon Hull City Transport. Park Royal took over Crossley's share of Birmingham's business, bodying half of its orders for Daimler Fleetlines. Roe also had the questionable privilege of being the main bodybuilder on Guy's ill-starred Wulfrunian double-decker of 1959-65.

ACV and MCW were gradually being chased by Alexander, which won orders from Newcastle Corporation and the Northern General group for

Above:
Duple (and Leyland) seemed safe and secure when this Dominant-bodied Tiger was delivered to Southend Transport. Quality problems and fast model changes contributed to Duple's demise. *Stewart J. Brown*

Below:
Eastern Coach Works depended to a large extent on the state-owned fleets for its business. One of its more colourful customers was Highland Scottish. This is a Daimler Fleetline. *Stewart J. Brown*

Right:
The final design of ECW body was developed for the Leyland Olympian chassis. This PMT example was built in the days of the National Bus Company. The design is still in production at the Leyland Bus Workington plant.
Stewart J. Brown

an MCW-like Atlantean body in 1958, but its real leap forward came in 1962 when the industry had become more design conscious.

The MCW, Roe and Alexander bodies on early Atlanteans and Fleetlines had all the design finesse of a lump of lard; square corners, flat windscreens, shallow top deck windows. Alexander had incorporated curved front and rear windscreens into its Y-type single-decker in 1961, and, to meet Glasgow Corporation's demand for a more revolutionary body for the Atlantean, used them on the front of the double-decker.

It was a huge success and helped get Alexander into more BET fleets, winning Trent from MCW and even getting in, with modifications, to Midland Red which still built some of its own bodies and chassis at its Carlyle works in Birmingham.

MCW agreed to fit Alexander windscreens and glassfibre mouldings to its Orion-derived body, initially for Newcastle, and Alexander windscreens became options on Roe, East Lancs and Northern Counties bodies. MCW had to depart further from its standard body for Liverpool, which specified equal depth windows and peaked roof domes for 379 1962-67 Atlanteans. Similar styling went into East Lancs's first Atlanteans bodies, supplied to Bolton in 1962.

A bodybuilder could adapt to changing tastes and styles, but MCW's market dominance was dealt a more savage blow in 1962. ACV 'merged'

with Leyland – in other words it was taken over – and Leyland regained its own bodybuilding capacity for the first time in eight years. Three years later, Bristol and ECW returned to the open market with Leyland taking a 25% stake in exchange for the Transport Holding Company buying a similar share in Park Royal and Roe.

It was with Park Royal, no longer MCW, that Leyland would pursue new business at home and abroad. The Weymann factory closed in 1965.

Duple grew in the 1950s, first moving its all-metal bus production from Hendon to Leicestershire after it bought Nudd Brothers & Lockyer of Kegworth and renamed it Duple (Midland). Then, in 1958, it bought Loughborough-based Willowbrook which, along with MCW, Alexander and Park Royal, enjoyed a share of the BET group's orders for steel-framed buses and coaches.

Then, in 1960 it bought arch rival Burlingham, renamed it Duple (Northern), and continued to produce separate ranges of products in Blackpool, the Midlands and London. But Burlingham's bus building work – it had supplied Manchester and

Below:
Glasgow Corporation had a major influence in reshaping double-deck bus bodies, encouraging Alexander to fit curved windscreens. The first of the new-style bodies on Leyland Atlantean chassis were delivered in 1962. It helped Alexander find even more English customers.
Stewart J. Brown

Ribble with 266 double-deckers between 1955 and 1958 – came to an end.

MCW and Park Royal both made valiant attempts to sell coach bodies in the 1960s, mainly to BET companies like Southdown and East Kent, but could not rival the coach specialists and another of those, Harrington, pulled out of coach manufacturing in 1965 and handed over its parts and service work to Plaxton.

By then, Plaxton had emerged from the shadows. Its Panorama body, with long side windows, had been launched in 1958 to meet the needs of a BET operator, Sheffield United Tours, and was developed progressively through the 1960s, picking up some big fleet business, until 1968, when it was transformed into the trend-setting curved-sided Panorama Elite.

Its launch coincided with massive upheaval at Duple which transferred all coach production to Blackpool in 1969 and streamlined its range, but not sufficiently to counter the Plaxton threat and it was ousted for ever from market leadership.

Duple shrunk further in 1971 when managing director George Hughes left and bought

Below:
Harrington's 1960s designs were stylish, but as Duple and Plaxton gained strength Harrington decided to pull out. Ribble received 22 Harrington-bodied Leyland Leopards in 1963 which were sold in the early 1970s. Five found their way to the Jones of Aberbeeg fleet. *A. D. Broughall*

Willowbrook back out of the group as an independent company which tried to break back into the coach market.

The upheaval of the 1960s was not confined to the coach market. Operators started demanding ever different types of buses, creating opportunities for new players to enter the market, and the Wilson Government changed just about everything else – the structure and funding of the operating and manufacturing industries.

New Construction and Use regulations legalised 11m single-deckers in 1961, making it possible to seat 53 passengers in a single-decker. You could get the same number in an old lowbridge double-decker and only three more in a typical immediate postwar double-decker. Suddenly many operators looked very seriously at single-deckers.

To begin with, the chassis were better suited to interurban and smaller town work. Mid-underfloor-engined models like the Leyland Leopard and AEC Reliance appealed to the bigger company operators in the BET and Scottish Bus groups and to some smaller municipalities, but the low floor Bristol/ECW RE was developed for the THC companies in 1962 and the open market got the RE in 1965, the year after the equivalent Daimler Roadliner, Leyland Panther/Panther Cub and AEC Swift appeared.

Alexander met the Scottish market's needs with its new Y-type which was built in bus, coach and semi-coach forms and met with some limited

Above:
Willowbrook's position in the body-building industry has changed dramatically. In 1965 it was still big enough to win fleet orders from major operators, including London Transport who ordered a batch of BET-style bodies on AEC Reliance chassis for Green Line operation as seen here at Aldgate coach station in 1974. *Stewart J. Brown*

Below:
Marshall has vanished from the body-building business. Its final design was the striking Camair 80, seen here on a Dennis Dominator in the Chester fleet. This bus was new to Merthyr Tydfil Transport. *Stewart J. Brown*

appeal in other markets. The BET companies laid down strict design criteria for their single-deck buses and by 1963 this included double curvature front and rear windscreens and peaked roof domes.

MCW and Park Royal shared in this business, but it was Willowbrook and a newcomer to the market, Marshall of Cambridge, which did best. Marshall's first BET buses were Reliances supplied to City of Oxford in 1961 and it went on to have sporadic successes in the bus market.

Pennine Coachcraft, Seddon's bodybuilding division, bodied Seddon and other single-deck chassis and Strachans, a long-established firm, re-entered the market in 1962 from premises at Hamble, near Southampton and achieved short-lived success with single-deckers. Its greatest coup was an order for London Transport's first 11m low floor single-decks, 15 Swift-derived AEC Merlins built in 1966.

London's subsequent bus orders – for its ill-fated Bus Reshaping Plan – helped seal MCW's fate. It ordered 650 Merlins for 1968/69, and 838 10m Swifts for 1969-72 delivery.

MCW won the entire Merlin body orders at the same time as it was bodying 110 Panthers for Liverpool and overstretched itself so much that some of the last Orion-family bodies – Leyland PD3s for Brighton and Atlanteans for Devon General – had to be completed by Cammell Laird at the old Saunders-Roe factory in Anglesey, and other customers like Bournemouth and Newcastle turned to Alexander for future orders.

Liverpool also changed allegiance, mainly to Alexander, but also to East Lancs, and MCW never made up the ground it lost by winning the London order. It got 46% of the body order for London Swifts, sharing it with Park Royal and Marshall and got only one-third of London's double-deck orders – Park Royal got the rest – when it bought 2,646 Fleetlines between 1970 and 1978.

The big provincial operators wanted new shapes of double deckers by 1968/69. Manchester persuaded Park Royal, Roe, MCW and East Lancs to produce a custom-built double-deck design, the Mancunian, on Atlanteans and Fleetlines from 1968. This was designed for one-man operation, had bigger windows, even translucent ceiling panels to brighten the upper deck.

It was toned down for the mass market, with Park Royal/Roe and MCW developing a similar design with more rounded edges, but deep windows and a four-bay construction which became the new shape for the 1970s – even in London.

While all this was going on, the 1968 Transport Act brought the BET and THC companies together under the National Bus Company and reformed the municipal undertakings of the West Midlands, Greater Manchester, Tyneside and Merseyside into passenger transport executives (PTEs). West and South Yorkshire got their PTEs in 1974.

NBC and Leyland then each had a half stake in Bus Manufacturers Holdings, a new holding company for ECW, Park Royal, Roe, Bristol, and

Below:
BET's standard single-deck bus and dual-purpose body was built by a number of makers. Willowbrook, as well as building for BET operators, supplied 14 BET-style bodies to London Transport in 1965 for Green Line operation. One is seen in the early 1970s after transfer to London Country Bus Services. *Stewart J. Brown*

Bottom:
Eastern Coach Works fulfilled the bulk of the National Bus Company's bus body orders. The company was jointly owned by NBC and Leyland. Crosville Bristol VRTs illustrate the NBC standard double-decker. *Stewart J. Brown*

Leyland National, a new company formed to build integral single-deckers at Workington.

From then, NBC had a vested interest in keeping the BMH plants busy, an interest more vital after the Leyland National went into production in 1971 and Bristol and ECW lost their orders for REs. ECW-bodied Bristol VRTs, still using a body clearly descended from ECW's early post-war double-deck design, were bought wherever possible, with Park Royal, Roe and ECW filling most of the gaps with Atlanteans. ECW also bodied large numbers of Bristol LH, even some Fords, for rural services.

Duple, Plaxton and Willowbrook supplied coaches, even some buses, but Northern Counties and Alexander lost much of the business they had built up with BET companies in the 1960s.

Northern Counties had bought its smaller neighbours in Wigan, Massey Brothers, taking it into Southend, Burton-on-Trent, Birkenhead, Chester, Caerphilly and Maidstone, but its real triumph came on its doorstep.

The SELNEC – later Greater Manchester – PTE brought together 11 operators with a wide range of vehicle specifications. The scope for standardisation was immense. It seized it with a vengeance and drew up a standard specification for double-deckers, based on the four-bay shape already being built for other operators. Park Royal built 360 on Atlantean and Fleetline chassis between 1972 and 1978, but Northern Counties ended up bodying 1,478 over a 12-year period, including a few built on other chassis being tried out by the PTE.

This business was won at the expense of the suppliers to the old municipalities – East Lancs, Roe, Pennine and, most notable of all, MCW.

But Northern Counties was squeezed out of other PTEs, Merseyside placing its business with Alexander, East Lancs and MCW, and West Midlands continued Birmingham's policy of splitting orders between Park Royal and MCW, West Yorkshire PTE carried over Leeds' Roe policy and South Yorkshire divided most of its business between Alexander and Roe.

East Lancs had been breaking into new markets throughout the 1960s, and, like Alexander, was gnawing away at MCW's customers. It supplied Coventry from 1966 until West Midlands took over in 1974, Brighton from 1975, Blackpool from 1977 and, along with Northern Counties, satisfied Nottingham's requirements for bespoke-bodied buses quite unlike anyone else's. East Lancs had evolved its body styling from the trendsetting Bolton buses, but offered many options to meet individual needs.

It was helped by the double-decker's rapid return to favour in the late 1960s, for the independent bodybuilders might have been in greater trouble had Leyland realised its dream of building up to 2,000 Nationals a year at Workington, using prefabricated construction methods imported from the car industry. That, added to the capacity of its three conventional body plants, would have left little room for others.

As it was, the other bodybuilders knew it would only be a matter of time before Leyland produced a double-deck equivalent of the National. MCW formed a new allegiance with Scania and imported its BR111 single-decker in 1969, gave the Swedish body design a British front end and marketed it as the Metro-Scania. This aroused sufficient interest for 133 to be bought over four years, and was developed in 1973 into a double-deck version, the integral Metropolitan.

Below:
To escape Leyland's monopoly on chassis supply, MCW formed links with Scania. One outcome was the Metropolitan double-decker. London Transport bought 164.
Stewart J. Brown

Above:
East Lancs, the first builder to body the Dennis Dominator, found new customers as a result. Scottish independents AA and A1 both bought East Lancs-bodied Dominators.
Stewart J. Brown

This had an entirely British body, similar in shape to MCW's standard double-deck body, and 660 were sold over the next five years, taking MCW back into some of its lost markets like Leeds, Glasgow, Merseyside and Tyne & Wear as well as into some new ones like Reading. It even sold 164 to London Transport, to go with six Metro-Scanias.

These were crazy times. The Government's new bus grant scheme meant Whitehall picked up half the tab for new vehicles and the industry went mad, buying more vehicles than the factories could build. Leyland's monopoly of the chassis market was ripe for a challenge and MCW could not fail in the short term. But the Metropolitan had mechanical problems and, worse for a coachbuilder, the bodies were prone to corrode.

To save itself, MCW transformed itself into a complete vehicle builder. It replaced the Swedish chassis units with its own Metrobus chassis and designed out much of the Metropolitan's corrosion trouble. So confident was MCW of its new future that it ceased bodying other chassis in 1979, the last being Atlanteans for Tyne & Wear.

Alexander and Northern Counties had less to worry about, especially as Leyland was prepared to let them build its new Titan double-decker for the Scottish and Manchester markets, but they were taking no chances.

Alexander co-operated with Ailsa Bus, the Volvo importer, to develop a body for its front-engined double-decker launched in 1973. The chassis shortage helped get 115 Ailsas into West Midlands and South Yorkshire and got Alexander into West Midlands, but Alexander was suffering from MCW's problems of a few years earlier and lost two South Yorkshire body orders. The Ailsas were built by Van Hool McArdle, the short-lived Belgian/Irish company set up to supply the Irish bus market, and MCW picked up a Fleetline order.

Alexander could call on additional production capacity at its Northern Ireland factory, owned since 1969 and linked with the company for a lot longer. It built mainly for Ulster operators, but from 1974 to 1980 was responsible for a bus-before-its-time, the S-type integral 27-seater based on Ford's A-Series light truck.

Northern Counties persuaded Foden, the Cheshire truck manufacturer, to develop a rear-engined underframe which appeared in 1976 as the Foden-NC. Only seven were bodied, six by Northern Counties.

East Lancs bodied the seventh Foden, but its chance came the following year when Dennis announced its rear-engined Dominator double-decker. Alexander, Willowbrook and Northern Counties also bodied them, but the Dominator took East Lancs into such new markets as Leicester, Hull, Tayside and Bournemouth.

The Dominator also brought a new wave of business for Marshall which not only bodied single-deck versions, but built its first double-deck bodies on Leicester vehicles in 1978 and found a niche in the double-deck market over the next six years.

Leyland eventually got the Titan double-decker into production at Park Royal, but labour troubles held back production and Park Royal closed in 1980, after building only 273 Titans, most of them for London Transport. Leyland had the huge embarrassment of having to persuade major customers like London, the PTEs, NBC and the Scottish Bus Group either to buy alternative models or go elsewhere.

Elsewhere, for many, was MCW which had put the Metrobus into production in remarkably quick

time. Leyland never sold another double-decker to West Midlands and, for a time, MCW was London Transport's only double-deck supplier, ending up building over 1,400 for service in the capital.

A Mark 2 version was launched in 1982, with 60% fewer body parts and making use of pre-drilled sections for assembly by semi-skilled labour – a huge breakthrough for a still highly conservative bodybuilding industry.

With Park Royal closed, Leyland began to make better sense of its bodybuilding capacity. It tried to move Titan production to ECW, but the workforce turned it down. Production resumed in 1981 at Workington, where it probably ought to have been built all along, but the Titan died four years later, after London had placed all of its business that year with MCW.

Park Royal's conventional bodybuilding was transferred to Roe, which joined ECW in building Titan-derived Leyland bodies for the new Olympian double-decker launched in 1980. This bus was also bodied by Alexander, Northern Counties, East Lancs and Marshall. Roe returned to the coach market from 1982-84, building bodies for Leyland's rear-engined Royal Tiger Doyen, but the old problem of bus builders making coaches blighted this project and production soon moved to Workington.

By 1983, many of the decisions of the 1960s were being unmade. The National Bus Company was on the brink of privatisation and the new bus grant scheme was ending. That year, NBC sold its half share in BMH to Leyland, freeing itself, in principle, from any obligation to buy Leyland buses in future. Some NBC companies placed orders with MCW for Metrobuses and, most

Above:
The 1980s saw the demise of Duple. The attractive new Caribbean, launched in 1982, found a number of buyers but was short-lived. This Leyland Tiger was operated by Cavalier of Hounslow. *Stewart J. Brown*

significantly, for the double-deck Metroliner coach launched in 1982.

Leyland's losses went on mounting and Roe shut in 1984, leaving ECW to meet all the group's orders for Olympian bodies. Three years later, after Leyland Bus was sold to its management, ECW closed and its jigs and designs were transferred to Workington where Olympian body production resumed the following year.

Below:
Roe closed in 1984, but the factory was reopened by Optare in 1985 and soon had some exciting new products. First was the CityPacer, built on an uprated MAN-VW LT truck chassis. Two Cambus examples leave central Cambridge. *Stewart J. Brown*

The coach market was feeling a far more bitter wind. Imported bodywork, by Salvador Caetano of Portugal, first appeared in Britain in 1968. Belgian builders Van Hool and Jonckheere arrived soon after and, as the choice of imported products grew, British operators demanded higher standards of Plaxton, Duple and Willowbrook.

Duple had switched to all-metal construction with its Dominant of 1972, a body which owed its styling to Plaxton's Panorama Elite, and Plaxton had phased out composite bodies by 1978, but neither manufacturer enjoyed the happiest reputation for quality.

Willowbrook, beaten by NBC engineers' resistance to its final range of coaches and by problems in the export market, collapsed in the early 1980s, but returned in 1985 as a much smaller-scale supplier of new bodies for reconditioned chassis.

It was not alone in hitting trouble, Duple's Caribbean and Laser models flopped when they were launched in 1982 and the company was nearly bankrupt when it was bought the following year by the Hestair group, owner of Dennis. The entire range was replaced and the Integral 425 coach launched within two years, but the odds remained stacked against Duple.

The break-up of the National Bus Company left it without much of its past fleet business and Trinity Holdings, the management team which bought Hestair's vehicle businesses early in 1989, took only months to sell the coach designs to Plaxton.

Plaxton had changed considerably. It had bought Reeve Burgess, the Derbyshire small bus bodybuilder, in 1980 and in 1987 was taken over by the management of the Kirkby motor group. It went on to buy a French coachbuilder, Carrosserie Lorraine, from Iveco - Fiat's commercial vehicle division – in 1988 and minibus builder Mellor Coachcraft of Rochdale came as part of a larger motor group acquisition in 1989.

But it was still being battered by the seasonal nature of the coach market and, as well as entertaining plans of exporting coaches to Europe, it planned an assault on the bus market from 1991, starting with the aluminium-framed Verde single-decker and getting into double-deckers later.

But deregulation, privatisation and continuing high interest rates made life hell for bus manufacturers from the mid-1980s onwards.

Minibuses – bought by the thousand from 1984 onwards – changed the picture, too. Dormobile, Mellor and Reeve Burgess were among the earlier bodybuilders which converted Ford, Mercedes-Benz, and later Freight Rover parcel vans into minibuses. Then, NBC engineering companies like Carlyle (the old Midland Red works) and PMT Engineering got into the act.

The buses started getting bigger and demanded coachbuilt bodies. New specialists like Robin Hood joined the converters in this sector and Alexander, Northern Counties and East Lancs – starved of orders for big vehicles – produced minibuses.

Minibuses helped an old company come back to life. A new company, Optare, reopened the Roe factory in Leeds in 1985, initially with orders for midibuses from West and South Yorkshire PTEs, later with a few orders for Olympian bodies which Leyland was unable to supply between closing ECW and resuming production at Workington.

But Optare's great step forward was the 1986 launch of its stylish 25-seater CityPacer minibus based on a Volkswagen LT van chassis. This was designed as a bus from the start and led to a range of ever-larger buses.

MCW followed Optare into the purpose-built midibus market and in 1986 unveiled its 25 and 33-seat integral Metrorider, an integral midibus built to bus standards, and 600 were ordered within two years.

Duple also had a late role as midibuses also got bigger. It designed a distinctive body for Dennis's new rear-engined Dart, using the Cromweld welding techniques in the 425 coach. Plaxton developed its own Reeve Burgess Pointer body for the Dart, and Duple sold its design to Carlyle, which took over production in 1990. By then, Wadham Stringer, which had enjoyed short-lived success in the full-size single-deck bus market in the early 1980s, and Wrights of Ballymena, a small Ulster firm, were also in the Dart market.

The big bus builders had few troubles to seek. Northern Counties, owned 75% by Greater Manchester PTE from 1983, was being let down by its majority shareholder and biggest customer; Greater Manchester Buses, the PTE-owned bus company, needed fewer buses after deregulation and stopped buying double-deckers.

The other major players all ended up with new owners by 1990. The John Brown engineering group sold East Lancs to Drawlane Transport, one of the emerging buyers of privatised NBC companies, in 1987, opening up new opportunities to supply its bodies to former NBC companies in the Midlands, North-West England and the Home Counties.

The Alexander family sold its interest in the diverse industrial group, which included the Scottish and Ulster coachbuilding works, in 1990. Plaxton wanted to buy it to consolidate its move into the bus market, but institutional investors kept the complete group in Scottish hands.

Plaxton also had ambitions for part of the
biggest sale of 1989, the Laird group's sale of
MCW and its Metro-Cammell railway business.
MCW had not recouped the heavy cost of
developing five new product ranges – Metrobus
Mk1, Mk2, Metroliner coaches (double-deck and
single-deck), Metrorider and Metrocab London
taxi – in less than 10 years. Nor had it put enough
effort into build quality. And Laird had lost out in
its final survival gamble – its bid to buy Leyland
Bus in 1986.

Plaxton was interested in building the Metrobus
body at Scarborough, but its talks fell through.
Instead, Optare bought the Metrorider and the
Metrobus body, the chassis going to DAF.
Metrorider production restarted within months,
but the Metrobus body was re-engineered to use
Alusuisse framing and was relaunched in 1991.

That deal fitted further into place in 1990 after
Optare was sold to United Bus, the DAF-owned
Dutch company which had been buying up Dutch
and Danish bus and coach manufacturers.

In a shrunken and fragmented market, the
surviving bodybuilders have had to tap new
markets to survive. Alexander had been exporting
double-deckers to the Far East from the mid-
1970s and, after Park Royal, Roe and ECW
disappeared, it could claim to be the world's
biggest manufacturer of double-deckers.

At home, it has sold to some privatised NBC
companies (notably the Scottish-owned
Stagecoach group), ex-PTE companies and parts
of London Buses and independent operators

providing tendered services for London Transport.
But the Scottish Bus Group, its original customer,
dried up as a source of business from 1988 as it
faced privatisation and break-up. Its Ulster bodies
began to find more sales in Britain.

Northern Counties cheated oblivion with great
determination and sold into ex-NBC, ex-PTE and
London operators. It won some Merseybus orders
from Alexander and scored a further coup over its
Scottish rival in 1990 by recruiting its sales
director. But a project to body French-built
Renault PR100 single-deckers seemed doomed
after only five were built.

Leyland, under Volvo ownership from 1988, has
had a smaller slice of the bodywork market. Its
Olympians have gone to ex-NBC and London
operators while its Lynx single-decker, successor
to the National from 1985, has enjoyed wider
appeal. Leyland built all Lynx bodies until 1990,
but Plaxton and Alexander were both expected to
body it from 1991.

With such change behind them, it would be
comforting to think that the worst is over and that
the future is rosy. It is not.

With double-deckers becoming less popular,
Continental competitors could be attracted to the
British bus market. And in the longer term,
design standards could be brought closer to the
expectations of the automotive industry. Plaxton
has invested heavily in computer-aided design,
calculating stress factors and the likely impact of
long life on future body designs, but future
legislation could demand even higher standards
and transform the face of bodybuilding.

In that sort of regime there will be room only for
the few companies with the size and strength to
meet those standards. One or two of today's firms
may bridge that gap, but it is hard to believe that
they all will. Sad, but probably true.

Brighton by bus

Photographer **Kevin Lane** *illustrates buses in Brighton in recent years.*

Above:
August 1979, and Brighton seafront at 7am before the holidaymakers are up and about. A Southdown Northern Counties-bodied Leyland Titan PD3 heads for Worthing. New in 1964, it was one of a batch of 25 which stil survived intact in 1979.

Left:
In 1972 Southdown received 15 Daimler Fleetline CRL6s with highbridge Eastern Coach Works bodywork. One leaves a seafront stop in 1980, shortly before the entire batch was transferred to Crosville.

Above left:
Part of Southdown's training fleet in 1982. A Park Royal-bodied Titan PD2 stands alongside a trio of 1967 PD3s with panoramic-windowed Northern Counties bodies.

Left:
Pool Valley bus station in June 1986. From left to right the buses are Bristol VRTs of Southdown and Hastings & District, and Mark 2 and Mark 1 Leyland Nationals of Southdown.

Below left:
The Brighton & Hove Bus & Coach Co was formed in 1986 to take over Southdown's Brighton area operations. Vehicles transferred from Southdown included this Bristol VRT and the Leyland National seen pursuing it in June 1988.

Right:
Brighton & Hove's first new vehicles were minibuses, including 14 Iveco-Ford 49.10s with 21-seat Robin Hood bodies.

Below:
After privatisation Brighton & Hove standardised on Scania double-deckers. East Lancs supplied the bodywork. The White Horse Tavern at Rottingdean provides a backdrop.

Above left:
Brighton Borough Transport's standard 1970s double-decker was the East Lancs-bodied Leyland Atlantean. A 1977 example passes the Clock Tower in 1990. The 1977 delivery was the last built to two-door layout.

Left:
Bedford's JJL midibus never progressed beyond the prototype stage. Three were operated by Brighton and in 1986 were used on the Churchill Square shuttle service, in a livery of white and shades of orange.

Below:
Four 1968 PD3 Titans had their Metro-Cammell bodies converted to open top in the late 1970s. The injunction to 'Hop on, hop off' has failed to entice many customers in this 1990 view.

Widening horizons

There's more to life than London Transport,
Tony Neuls describes how he found this out.

Before I moved to Cheltenham in 1972 I lived in Bromley in Kent, and up until then I had given no consideration to buses outside London because I thought that they were not proper buses. I had bought my *British Bus Fleets: London Buses* each year, marked off what I had seen, and had taken photographs of London Transport – only!

However, before I left the Metropolis I started to notice that I was taking sideways glances at other buses and coaches like Southdown, Maidstone & District and East Kent. Then, the day after Boxing Day in 1971, my wife and I went down to Brighton for the day, and whilst suffering a leaking head-gasket on my dear old Fiat 850, I noticed that the Brighton Hove & District Bristol Lodekkas had started to appear in Southdown's apple green and cream livery, so I actually took some photographs of them. I had noticed over the years that these were rather special vehicles anyway as they had

Below:
Still in pre-NBC livery, a Sheffield United AEC Reliance at Cheltenham on the South West Clipper.

an LT-red RT used as a demonstrator by Fischertechnik Toys. Their familiar tones were like music to my ears among all those strange-sounding Gardners, Leylands and Bristols, but curiosity gradually turned my prejudices to an overall devotion and my present industry-wide interest.

My forays into the centre of Cheltenham from my new-found residence in the suburb of Hatherley (formerly known as *Up* Hatherley, because there was a *Down* version too) eventually took me to Cheltenham coach station, an enigma which exceeded my wildest dreams, because far from being in the sticks, I had discovered a gold-mine of coaches. There were a few names I had heard of like Red & White, Oxford/South Midland, Hants & Dorset, and even Southdown.

I knew all about, well, nearly all about, Royal Blue because many years before, back in the 1950s, I had travelled with my mother to see some friends in Frome by coach and we had travelled down from Victoria in an ersatz Royal Blue, actually an independent (heaven knows who) duplicating the Royal Blue service coach. On the way back, we got a real Royal Blue which I now believe to have been one of the Duple-bodied Bristol LLs, but at the time it left me unmoved.

Reverting to Cheltenham there were lots of strange names including Black & White who I am

the London Tranport-type flashing indicators fitted to the front corners, and from that day, the widening of my horizons had started.

The move to Cheltenham actually happened in August 1972 and I was lucky enough to arrive there when everything was still Cheltenham red and cream and Tilling green and cream, and there were some apparently interesting (I know better now!) Bristol KSWs. However, for a while I found solace in Harry's Coaches former Jersey Motor Transport RTLs with their re-imported J-suffix registrations, the Warners of Tewkesbury two-tone green RTs, a caravan-converted RF down the Bristol Road in Gloucester and a fleeting visit of

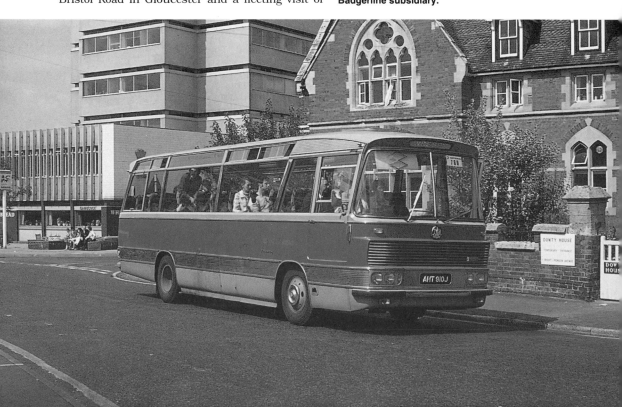

now ashamed to admit I had not really noticed before, and others like Lincolnshire, Northern General, Crosville, Ribble, Stratford Blue, Western Welsh (who I subsequently discovered should really have been Eastern Welsh), and the delightfully parochial Jones of Aberbeeg with a very impressively kept fleet and, of course, many others.

I soon got to know the delights of Cheltenham's interchange with its two o'clock mass departure, when the bell rang on the dot of 2pm, and up to 100 vehicles started up together, sealed off St Margarets Road and roared off in all directions to every part of the isle from Penzance to Pwllheli, Edinburgh to Eastbourne and Carlisle to Clacton.

In January 1984, the famous two o'clock departures ceased, giving way to just a trickle of coaches throughout the day and Cheltenham sadly was a major interchange no more. Even more sadly, Cheltenham coach station subsequently closed altogether, after a small revival in 1985 when the local Cheltenham District buses moved from their depot at St Marks and joined what coaches were left. Even the buses left on 12 January 1986 and took the coaches with them to a refurbished depot at St Marks, leaving just the few daily services passing through until closure, leaving a large gap in the town's way of life.

Over the years, I was well and truly converted from my London-only interest and would get really excited with a new Bristol RE or an old MW, or somebody's new Leopard or Tiger, and I saw all

sorts of chassis and body manufacturers represented there with vehicles from just about every National Bus Company subsidiary (except Gateshead and District, and the nearby Tyneside), plus many, many independents, local authorities and passenger transport executives and took thousands, yes thousands of colour slides and spent many exciting hours there.

My interest extended to gaining a PSV driver's licence and indulging in some weekend driving for

Black & White for some years when I got to know, and gain a strong affection for the Leyland Leopard, both manual and semi-automatic. The 02.30 night service to Exmouth was my favourite, duplicating back on the 08.30 Royal Blue service, driving through some delightful country, down through Lyme Regis, Seaton, Beer, Sidmouth, Newton Poppleford (what a lovely name), Budleigh Salterton and into Exmouth, returning home through Sidmouth, then over the top to Honiton, over again to Cullompton, a bacon sandwich in Taunton, then Bridgwater, Highbridge, Burnham-on-Sea and Cheltenham. With these stops it was worth taking a camera especially with AEC Regent Vs at Exmouth, and of course there were the two o'clocks waiting for you when you got back.

In concluding the history of my conversion I have ferreted through my logbooks and list here my log at the coach station, Cheltenham for Saturday 3 August 1974. It does not include Black & White, because I had got them all, and the regular East Yorkshire and Yelloways coaches for the same reason, but it does include Wessex of Bristol while still independent, several NBC companies not now with us and even some which went and have come back again. Happy days.

Table

Operator	Registration	Chassis	Body
Cavalier, Hounslow	ORO 312M	Seddon Pennine VI	Panorama Elite III
Shamrock & Rambler 4111	DRU 970L	Bedford YRO	Dominant
Sheffield United Tours 358	EWJ 358C	AEC Reliance	Panorama I
Midland Red 5779	CHA 79C	Leopard PSU3/4R	Duple Commander
Midland Red 315	PHA 315M	Leopard PSU3B/4RT	Panorama Elite III
Greenslades 442	AFJ 77B	AEC Reliance 2MU4RA	Harrington
Hants & Dorset 1019	FRU 874D	Bristol MW6G	ECW
Ribble 1034	XTF 808L	Leopard PSU3B/4R	Dominant
United Counties 286	WBD 286H	Bristol RELH6G	ECW
Northern 2634	FCN 634F	Leopard PSU3/4R	Alexander Y
Sheffield United 366	KWE 366D	AEC Reliance	Panorama I
Sheffield United 405	DWA 405H	AEC Reliance	Panorama Elite
National Travel North East	YWE 494M	Bedford YRT	Dominant
National Travel North East	YWE 505M	Bedford YRT	Dominant
Wallace Arnold	VUB 396H	Leopard PSU3A/4R	Panorama Elite
Ribble 1023	WTF 569L	Leopard PSU3B/4R	Dominant
Ribble 1015	PTF 710L	Bristol RELH6L	ECW
National Travel North East	MHD 772L	Leopard PSU3B/4R	Panorama Elite III
Harding's, Wirral	JBG 500F	AEC Reliance	Panorama I
Harding's, Wirral	GCM 100F	AEC Reliance	Panorama I
Charnwood Coaches	KJU 39L	Bedford YRQ	Dominant
Whittle 23	PNT 733M	Bedford YRT	Dominant
Matthews, Churchdown 31	BUX 220L	Bedford YRQ	Dominant
Cottrell's, Mitcheldean	JOE 189E	AEC Reliance	Panorama I
Corvedale (Whittle) 47	BUX 237L	Bedford YRQ	Dominant
M & M (Whittle) 40	BUX 240L	Bedford YRT	Dominant
Thomas Bros, Llangadog	STH 200K	Ford R192	Viceroy Express
Midland Red 201	JHA 201L	Leopard PSU3B/2B	Marshall
Western Welsh UC369	OUH 175G	Leopard PSU3A/4RT	Panorama Elite
East Midland C62	262 PRR	Leopard PSU3/3RT	Panorama
WEMS, Weston 26	GUV 7D	Bedford VAL14	Vega Major
WEMS, Weston 7	591 NTT	Bedford SB	Bella Vega
Wallace Arnold	AUA 434J	AEC Reliance	Panorama Elite II

Richardson, Hartwell	DBD 28K	Ford R226	Panorama Elite II
WEMS, Weston 5	479 MBF	Bedford SB	Super Vega
Lincolnshire 1617	VVL 845M	Ford R1014	Dominant
Western Welsh UC165	DBO 152C	AEC Reliance 2MU4RA	Panorama I
Reliance of Newbury 137	JRL 552E	Bedford VAM14	Panorama I
Morley's of Edwinstowe	UAL 103L	Leopard PSU3B/4R	Dominant
Corvedale (Whittle) 46	BUX 236L	Bedford YRQ	Dominant
Premier Travel, Cambridge 189	GER 502E	AEC Reliance	Alexander Y
Godfrey Abbott, Sale	NMB 279L	Bedford YRQ	Dominant
Shamrock & Rambler 535	DRU 972L	Bedford YRT	Dominant
Sheffield United 378	OWA 378E	AEC Reliance	Panorama I
?	LUN 529F	Bedford VAM	Viscount
Western Welsh UC266	GKG 157D	AEC Reliance	Panorama I
Netherfield, Nottingham	FNR 9L	Ford R192	Panorama Elite III

(Mis-logged, should have been logged as N&S, Oadby – must have been the excitement!)

Royal Blue 1307	RDV 442H	Bristol LH6L	Duple Commander IV
Royal Blue 1407	745 MDV	Bristol MW6G	ECW
Yelloway	KDK 801F	AEC Reliance	Panorama I
Tillings 9415	YTW 539F	Bristol RESH6G	Duple
Red & White RD572	CWO 288K	Bristol RELH6G	ECW
Shamrock & Rambler 522	MEL 988F	Bedford VAL70	Viceroy
Yelloway	WDK 649K	AEC Reliance 6U3ZR	Panorama Elite II
Greenslades 466	EOD 26D	AEC Reliance 2U4RZ	Harrington Grenadier
M & M (Whittle) 39	BUX 239L	Bedford YRQ	Dominant
Scarlett, Minehead	HTF 447F	Bedford VAM14	Viceroy
Corvedale (Whittle) 47	BUX 237L	Bedford YRQ	Dominant
Wessex	ART 910J	Bedford YRQ	Viceroy
Silcox, Pembroke Dock 65	635 SDE	Leopard PSU3/3R	Duple Continental
Red & White DS759	UWO 707	Bristol MW6G	ECW
Scarlett, Minehead	NTT 135M	Bedford YRQ	Dominant
Midland Red 5826	GHA 326D	Leopard PSU4/4R	Panorama I
?	SVJ 936J	Bedford SB	Vega 31
?	RKJ 106G	Ford R226	Viceroy
Wallace Arnold	JUA 301E	Leopard PSU3/4R	Panorama I
Berry's, Taunton	YYC 230H	Bedford VAM70	Panorama Elite
Yelloway	TDK 687J	AEC Reliance 6U3ZR	Panorama Elite II
Weardon's, Farnworth	OTJ 198J	Ford R226	Panorama Elite II
Ribble 1031	XTF 805L	Leopard PSU3B/4R	Dominant
Whittle 19	BUX 219L	Bedford YRQ	Dominant
Ribble 1025	WTF 571L	Leopard PSU3B/4R	Dominant
Tynemouth 304	EFT 704F	Leopard PSU4/4R	Alexander Y
United 1244	NHN144F	Bristol RFLH6G	ECW
Greenslades 310	BFJ 310L	Bristol RELH6L	Panorama Elite III
Hants & Dorset 1022	FRU 877D	Bristol MW6G	ECW
Wessex	RHT 918G	Bedford VAM70	Viceroy
Bristol SD/2050	NHW 304F	Bristol RELH6L	ECW
Hill, Pershore	FNM 537E	Ford R192	Panorama I

Plus all the Black & Whites, Crosville and a Western SMT Leopard/Alexander on the Paignton-Glasgow service.

Above:
A rare visitor to Cheltenham: an Alexander-bodied Leyland Leopard from the Tynemouth fleet on service from Newcastle.

Right:
A new Ford R1014 with Duple Dominant body from the Lincolnshire fleet in National livery.

Below right:
Cheltenham & District's L8569 an ECW-bodied Bristol Lodekka.

Country bus

Rural bus services still serve much of out-of-the-way Britain. Intrepid photographer **John Burnett** scales remote peaks to photograph examples in the Lake District and Scotland.

Above:
This 1983 view of a Ribble Leyland National 2 running from Coniston to Ulverston illustrates the rural transport problem. The bus is empty.

Left:
There are not too many customers on this rural bus either, splashing towards Edinburgh as the snow melts around it. The bus is a Seddon Pennine with Alexander Y-type body, standard fare for Scottish Bus Group subsidiary Eastern Scottish in the late 1970s.

Above left:
Ribble operated Bristol REs until the late 1980s. An Eastern Coach Works-bodied example passes sheep and dry stone walls above Lake Coniston.

Left:
Most rural buses are single-deckers, especially in sparsely-populated areas. One exception is Ribble's Lancaster to Keswick service, seen here near Grasmere in 1988 being operated by a Park Royal-bodied Leyland Atlantean AN68.

Top:
An ex-London Transport short Bristol LHS/ECW approaches Kirkstone Pass in service with The Mountain Goat of Windermere. The Mountain Goat specialises in the operation of small buses on routes with tourist appeal.

Above:
A Ribble B-series Leyland National (with conventional heating in place of the roof-pod warm air curtain system) crests a gradient in the Lake District in the red, white and grey livery used before the company was taken over by Stagecoach in 1989. The bus was new in 1979.

Right:
The Cairngorm Chairlift Company operates this two-door Leyland National 2. It ferries employees and visitors to the bottom of the ski slopes where chairlift and ski-tows take them on to parts which even rural buses cannot penetrate.

Catalogues of disaster

Gavin Booth *considers bus manufacturers'
publicity material, with the emphasis on unfulfilled
expectations.*

It started when I was a mere lad. Every time I visited a Motor Show I returned with bags bulging with catalogues and other promotional material. I convinced my mother that I really had to keep them just in case, and now I try the same argument with my wife because the intervening years have changed nothing. I still return from the National Exhibition Centre or from press conferences with luggage that is considerably heavier than it was when I left home.

Bus and coach manufacturers have always believed in the power of promotional brochures; some, like AEC and Leyland, issued a glossy leaflet for every new model, indeed every model variation. Others restricted their efforts to simply-produced leaflets for distribution at Motor Shows.

As the manufacturing industry shrunk, companies that had previously adopted a low profile started to invest in glossy, full-colour publicity material, and brochure-collectors found themselves with examples from bodybuilders like Alexander and Northern Counties – although my collection still lacks anything from East Lancs, who never exhibit at the principal shows and seem to survive in spite of this.

There is a theory that the cost and glossiness of brochures is in inverse proportion to the success of the manufacturer. Certainly when Leyland was suffering from its various crises in the 1970s and early 1980s it produced some superb and apparently expensive material.

But did it all work? I have some manufacturers' brochures for models that never quite made it, and with the benefit of hindsight they make fascinating reading. At the time they were issued the sales team had everything they needed – glossy buses and glossy brochures – and everything must have seemed rosy.

After all, how were the brochure writers to know that no-one would want to buy their new bus, that the market might change, that the new model was a dud?

Take the **AEC Bridgemaster** as an example. A glossy full-colour booklet issued in 1958 trumpets the virtues of this integrally-built bus of advanced design and on paper it looks like a good idea. A chassisless low-height double-decker in the Bristol/ECW Lodekka mould with Routemaster features like a front sub-frame and independent suspension, and a 125bhp AEC engine.

But the Bridgemaster was not a success. In five years in production, only 179 were built, and its replacement, the Renown chassis, was only marginally more successful with a total build of 251.

So what went wrong? Operators were suspicious of integral construction; it took later models like the Leyland National and MCW Metrobus to change their minds. The advanced features led to reliability problems, and customers weren't ready for air suspension on the rear axle.

And AEC had misread the market for low-height double-deckers. While Bristol and ECW supplied the needs of the Tilling and Scottish groups with the Lodekka until 1968, the need for low-height buses was reducing, with many operators turning to high-capacity single-deckers in the 1960s. To crown it all, deadly rival Leyland had launched its rear-engined Atlantean double-deck chassis at the same time as the Bridgemaster, and at a stroke front-engined double-deckers looked dated.

One of the earliest brochures in my collection is for the **Dennis Dominant** chassis, and dates from 1950. This was a time of fresh hope in the bus

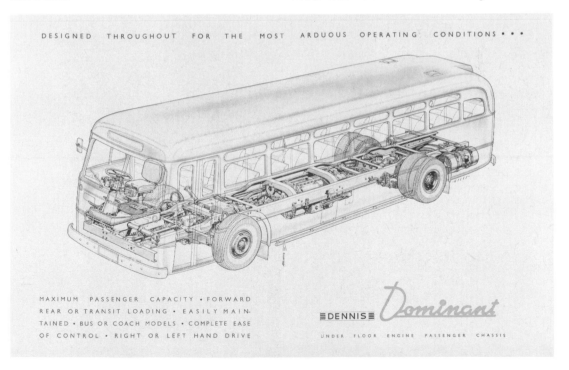

DESIGNED THROUGHOUT FOR THE MOST ARDUOUS OPERATING CONDITIONS • • •

MAXIMUM PASSENGER CAPACITY • FORWARD REAR OR TRANSIT LOADING • EASILY MAINTAINED • BUS OR COACH MODELS • COMPLETE EASE OF CONTROL • RIGHT OR LEFT HAND DRIVE

≡DENNIS≡ *Dominant*

UNDER FLOOR ENGINE PASSENGER CHASSIS

Rear Engined Silent Passenger Chassis

clue to Daimler's engine choice is given in the phrase 'the extremely compact dimensions of the power unit'; certainly it kept engine intrusion to a minimum, but did nothing else to endear the model to British operators. A Perkins V8 engine was offered in the Roadliner from 1968, and there was a last-ditch attempt to save the model with the Leyland (AEC) V8-800 the following year, but the damage had been done. Perhaps if Daimler had followed Bristol's example and shoe-horned the Gardner 6HLW in the rear, the Roadliner might today be discussed in the hushed tones reserved for the RE.

In fairness to Daimler, the early rear-engined single-deck models did not represent the bus industry's finest hour. A 1968 **Leyland Panther** brochure suggests that 'the chassis provides the answer to today's problems of passenger transportation, both in high density city centres or for the long strides of inter-continental coaching operation'. While it was not a disaster in the Roadliner league, the Panther was not the runaway success that Leyland had hoped for.

Nor did the **Seddon RU** set the heather on fire. The Oldham-based manufacturer sought to break into the UK citybus market with a chassis that offered the popular Gardner 6HLX engine, but total sales of around 250 were poor against the well-proved and long-running Bristol RE and Leyland Leopard.

Even **Volvo** failed to make an impact with its **B59** rear-engined bus chassis in 1972. Here was a model that was to prove successful in other parts

industry, with passenger figures at an all-time high, and new models appearing at regular intervals.

The fashion was the underfloor-engined single-decker and while most manufacturers chose to produce what were essentially flat-engined versions of their front-engined models, Dennis went further. The Dominator had a Hobbs semi-automatic transmission, a novelty at the time, providing for smooth gear engagement in spite of the engine revolutions being inaudible from the driver's cabin. In spite of this refinement, not yet offered on other chassis, the Dominant was a heavy chassis; only two were built before Dennis launched the simpler Lancet UF in 1953.

The **Daimler Roadliner** was another promising model. Daimler's reputation as bus-builders had been based on soundly-built chassis with reliable Gardner engines and Wilson preselector gearboxes. It was a major step to introduce a low-floor rear-engined model in 1964, and a calculated risk to fit an unfamiliar engine, the Cummins V6-200. A two-colour leaflet of the time says that the engine 'provides a wide range of power outputs and engine speeds with exceptional standards of performance and freedom from vibration'.

What it doesn't mention is that the engine's poor reliability dogged early Roadliners, and a

The Seddon Pennine R.U. Bus Chassis

of Europe, launched on the UK market in right-hand drive form. A demonstrator with Marshall bodywork was built and this features in a brochure of the time.

There was basically nothing wrong with the B59 except that the home market was not ready for it. Its UK launch coincided with the start of Leyland National production, and there was not the ready acceptance of imported buses that characterises the market today. The demonstrator remained the only B59 built for the UK.

Scania enjoyed greater success with an advanced rear-engined citybus when the **Metro-Scania** was on the market between 1970-73, but only 120 were sold. This collaboration with MCW was Scania's first attempt to break into the UK bus market, and the single-deck model was followed by the double-deck Metropolitan. A contemporary leaflet extols the virtues of noise reduction and promotes the Metro-Scania Quiet Bus with noise levels about 77dB(A).

MCW went on to specialise in building complete vehicles, most notably the Metrobus double-decker, but also dabbled in coach models in the 1980s without notable success. The **Metroliner** single-deck range comprised normal-height and Hi-Liner models, but these enjoyed only limited success with a small group of customers. The

listen to this

Some facts relating to vehicle noise and its reduction

METRO·SCANIA
THE "SILENT" BUS (noise level about 77 dB(A)) (Patents pending)

METROLINER 2-DECK

The 12-metre, 3 axle, 2-deck Metroliner coach, derived from the proven Metrobus 3-axle chassis, enables luxury travel to be provided at the lowest economic cost. Up to 86 seated passengers can be accommodated if the rear enclosed luggage area is not required. Even with provision of a 10.125 cubic metres interior luggage compartment, 82 seats can be utilised. The economic operating benefits possible with these high passenger loads can be considerable.

A variety of alternative interior layouts are available to suit most types of operation from high capacity express routes to top flight executive type services featuring all the luxuries, video, vending machines, toilets, tables and so on—exactly what would be expected from a product of premier quality.

The 2-deck Metroliner has a chassis underframe with integrated steel body structure with stretched steel exterior panelling and bonded windows. The engine used is the versatile rear-mounted Cummins diesel, developing 290 bhp, driving through a Voith automatic gearbox.

The driver has the benefit of fully comprehensive controls and dashboard layout, to ensure fatigue-free driving, even under the most arduous of circumstances. He and the passengers also benefit from superlative ride and handling characteristics through the air suspension and excellent on the road performance which renders possible precise timing of scheduled high speed journeys.

A notable characteristic of the Metroliner 2-deck is the generous headroom on both decks, made possible by its 4.23 metres overall height. Mechanical units, proven in arduous service, are designed for cost cutting, long life and trouble-free operation, with ease of access for efficient servicing and maintenance when eventually required. The unique combination of M.C.W. and established manufacturers of major units ensures a comprehensive spread of service and spare parts throughout the life of the vehicle.

The exterior and interior fittings and appointments and the range of optional extras available on the 2-deck Metroliner, are fully commensurate with the best standards achieved on deluxe single deck coaches, whilst Metroliner's overall appearance is impressive and highly prestigious, capable of forming the flagship of any operator's fleet.

double-deck Metroliner was altogether more successful in sales terms, particularly to National Bus Company and Scottish Bus Group fleets, but reliability problems led many customers to dispose of them prematurely.

A glossy brochure for the Metroliner coach range talks of 'Mechanical units, proven in arduous service . . . designed for cost-cutting, long life and trouble-free operation, with ease of access for efficient servicing and maintenance when eventually required', sentiments that several operators might challenge today.

I was surprised to find a **Bristol Lodekka** brochure in my collection. Surely Bristol, with its captive market of nationalised operators, did not need to publicise its wares? Yet here was a simply produced glossy leaflet promoting the 'new' flat-floor FS and FLF chassis. It is undated, and the flat-floor models first appeared in 1959, but a photo of a 1966 United FLF provides a clue, and a reminder that Bristol models were now available on the open market, and sales outside the nationalised sector may have been the motive. As it turned out, no Lodekkas were sold on the wider market, although the model continued in production until 1968, and subsequent plans for a semi-lowheight Lodekka chassis were aborted.

Considerably less successful was the **Foden-NC** double-deck chassis, first introduced in 1976 as

an alternative to the Daimler Fleetline, then in its last years. The combination of the Gardner 6LXB engine and Foden's reputation as truck builders could have produced a serious contender in the double-deck market, but the customers for the seven built did not come back for more, and

FODEN

001

SPECIAL

FODEN-NC

NORTHERN COUNTIES

BEDFORD

JJL Midi Bus

CITY CENTRE 024

changes in ownership in 1980 meant that Foden's enthusiasms were once more directed at the truck market.

The bus was a collaboration between Foden and coachbuilders Northern Counties, hence the model name, and sales enquiries were directed to Wigan rather than Sandbach – though there appeared to be precious few of them, and the bus quietly disappeared from the model lists.

If few mourned the Foden-NC, there were many who felt that the **Bedford JJL** was never really given a chance. Bedford had specialised in building truck-derived chassis for the lighter end of the bus and coach market, and in 1976 got involved with the Camuta design concept produced by Marshall, the Cambridge bodybuilders.

This was a neat and attractive rear-engined semi-integral midibus seating up to 27 passengers. Bedford's 1976 JJL brochure enthused that 'the JJL is indeed a thoroughbred PSV; its pedigree contains all the experience Bedford have gained in supplying the world with quality bus and coach chassis for over 45 years. It is brilliant in design, robust in construction, and engineered for long life . . . to maximise the operator's return on his investment.'

It featured an extremely low floor line and the spacious feel of a bigger bus, but in spite of early

enthusiasm Bedford, or its masters General Motors, took cold feet when full production was considered. The project was dropped in 1980 after a handful of prototypes had been built.

If anything the JJL was a decade ahead of its time. The UK bus industry was not ready for small buses, but the Dennis Dart and Optare Metrorider are the JJL's natural successors, and it is a pity that nobody was prepared to take the JJL concept forward.

If giant corporations are wary of investment in new models, it is sometimes easier for smaller builders to get started in the bus and coach market, though survival can be just as precarious.

Take two more recent entrants to the UK chassis market, **ACE** and **Quest 80**. Both had seen a gap in the model lists for bespoke chassis, and I discovered leaflets for the ACE Predator range and the various Quest 80 models.

The Huddersfield firm Alternative Chassis Engineering (ACE) was based on the erstwhile Ward company, and the Predator range comprised the Puma, Cheetah and Cougar chassis, although the coloured brochure does not explain which is which; the Puma was available with Perkins or DAF engines, and the Cheetah with the Perkins V8, all mid-mounted. The ACE has more recently resurfaced with plans for a rear-engined midibus.

THIS IS THE NEW

QUEST 80

MODEL D

The ultimate range of P.S.V. Chassis for PUMA, CHEETAH and COUGAR
Built by professionals · For professionals

ALTERNATIVE CHASSIS ENGINEERING

A series of leaflets for the Telford-built Quest 80 range shows the 'C' high-floor coach chassis and the 'D' bus chassis. The rear-engined C and D models had Ford 6-litre engines, and the C was available in 9, 11 and 12 metre lengths, and the D was an 8.7m midibus. Quest had been set up in 1979 and its major sales success was an order for 20 VM coach models for Excelsior of Bournemouth in 1984, but the order was never completed and the VM together with the C and D and Quest 80 vanished without trace.

The **Leyland Olympian** has been the most successful of the current generation of double-deck models, yet its success has not been universal. Leyland has long argued the virtues of the double-decker as a more efficient urban crowd-mover than the articulated single-deckers beloved of many cities. It has taken its argument to several countries with varying degrees of success, and in 1983 launched an assault on the United States market.

An ECW-bodied Olympian demonstrator was build to US specification and shipped out for use by transit authorities. With it went a glossy leaflet describing the Olympian as 'The Unexpected

Answer'. It argued that 'the double-deck bus is an ideal choice for the American transit industry', listing recent coverts like Ecuador, Greece, Indonesia, Kuwait, the Philippines and Singapore.

Why a double-decker? the leaflet asked. 'Passengers love the large number of seats and the low floor line. The upper deck is a magnet to new riders, eager to enjoy a unique panorama of their city'. Leyland also presented arguments on stability, with details of the UK tilt test, and a less convincing argument on height. 'At around 170 inches tall', the copy read, 'a double-decker is 45 inches higher than most buses or just 8 inches taller than many trucks. So overhead clearance problems can generally be avoided'.

It may have been the word 'generally', or perhaps a natural suspicion of anything so clearly different, but the US transit industry did not beat a path to Leyland's door looking for Olympians. A pity, really, because they would have been at least as reliable as many current US transit buses, and probably more fuel-efficient into the bargain. At the end of the day only Gray Line bought a batch for sightseeing work in San Francisco.

The Olympian would certainly have been a more prudent choice for US operators than the Grumman 870, a singularly unsuccessful US transit bus designed to compete with the market-leading RTS model. The 870 suffered major structural problems, but the Grumman company bravely bounced back wtih a new model, the **Grumman Metro**.

The president of the Grumman Flexible Corporation prefaced the glossy Metro brochure with a frank admission of the problems. 'It's no secret that there have been structural problems with the A-frame and engine cradle of our Model 870 coach', he wrote. 'That fact, and exaggerations of that fact, is common knowledge to all members of the bus industry'.

I suspect that few British manufacturers would be brave enough to admit their failures, preferring to sweep them under the carpet and move on to the next project – if indeed they were still in business.

How often are new models launched on the market on a heady mixture of enthusiasm and confidence, without the firm foundation of market research and product quality? The examples I have quoted were selected as vehicles that never quite reached their targets, and it is sobering to realise that AEC, Bedford, Daimler, Foden, MCW, Quest 80 and Seddon no longer build bus and coach chassis.

It could be argued that some of these models were doomed from the start, while others were the right bus at the wrong time. Whatever the case, often all that we have left to remind us of their existence is a few glossy brochures – or, if you listen to my wife, *far too many* glossy brochures.

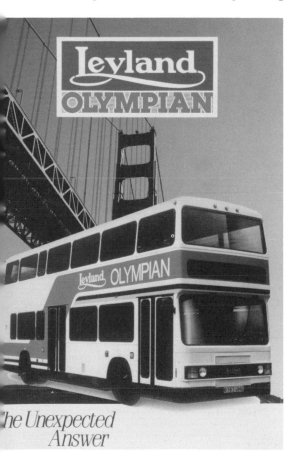

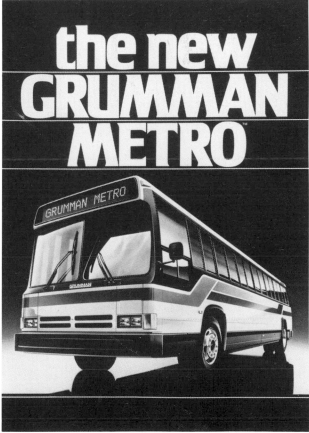

Potteries variety

Alastair Douglas *turns the clock back to scooters,
and variety at PMT.*

Many of my generation, when they pause to consider the follies of their youth, are surprised that they lived to tell the tale. In 1958 I became the proud owner of a brand-new Lambretta motor scooter which had a regrettable habit of transferring the oil from its transmission into the rear brakedrum. Despite several long sojourns on the premises of various dealers – even a four-month period while the Lambretta boffins down South drilled a very expensive breather hole which was supposed to cure the problem – it persisted in this annoying habit. On reflection perhaps it was as well it spent so much time off the road for, when it was available to me, my confidence in the coefficient of friction between shoe leather and tarmac was such that I continued to use it. But then, if I had not, I might not have discovered the Potteries until it was too late.

In 1959 I obtained a temporary job in Coventry and decided my masterpiece of Italian engineering was capable of getting me there from my home in Kilmarnock. In fact it did – after stranding me in Barnard Castle for three nights with a timing malfunction those who should know said just could not happen. It then spent a considerable time in dock in Rugby, but was restored to me before the annual holiday period came round. By then, no doubt due to its enforced inactivity, its front brake cable was seized. Undeterred I set forth for home, via the A6 instead of the A1 this time. This journey gave me my first glimpse of the remarkable bus fleet of the Potteries Motor Traction Co Ltd but, with the Preston bypass as almost the only motorway in existence and the ascent of the dreaded Shap Fell and the congestion in numerous towns en route still

facing me, I could not linger. However, I determined to return and see more as soon as possible. This I did shortly after my return to the Midlands.

The following year I set out on a tour of the country with a friend – by this time I at last had the sense to trade in the Lambretta for a Vespa which, apart from allowing itself to be stolen in Leeds, behaved perfectly – and naturally the planning had to include some time in Stoke-on-Trent. Outside PMT's depot there we bumped into a local enthusiast (not literally – my new mount

Below:
In 1943 and 1944 PMT received no less than 23 Guy Arabs with Strachan utility bodies. In 1952 many of them received new Northern Counties 8ft wide bodies as seen here in Stoke.

had brakes that actually worked, as did my friend's). That in itself was something of an event. Our ranks were much thinner then than today. What we could not have known then was that he was to become one of the better known municipal managers. Already many of the older buses which had caught my attention the previous year had gone but there was still plenty of variety.

The Potteries had long been a stronghold of independent operation but, in the post-war years, PMT had been rapidly buying out the opposition. Although several independents still survived in 1959, a great many more had been swallowed up. This rapid growth had created problems and,

between 1951 and 1954, large numbers of elderly double-deckers had been purchased from dealers. All of these had gone by 1959 but there were still lots of the buses and coaches taken over with the independents' businesses to be seen.

Below:
A further 10 Arabs delivered in 1946 had more durable Northern Counties bodies to a relaxed utility specification. This one was photographed in Newcastle-under-Lyme.

Bottom:
Among 1948 deliveries were 10 Daimler CVD6s with Burlingham bodywork. This one is seen outside the depot in Stoke.

Above:
One of 14 Leyland PS2/5 Tigers with Brush bodies delivered in 1950 was caught in Uttoxeter where the buses of Stevenson's and the Green Bus Company usually drew attention away from the PMT vehicles. Note the Ford Prefect.

Left:
1953 deliveries included 12 attractive AEC Regent III/Northern Counties like this one on service in Newcastle. The chassis of these vehicles had been ordered by Stoke-on-Trent Motors and Thomas Tilstone before they were taken over by PMT.

Below left:
Of the large fleet taken over with the Associated Bus Company's business in 1944 only three wartime 'deckers, two Daimlers and a Guy, survived in 1959 and these had been rebodied by Northern Counties in 1954. One of the Daimlers was found in service in Stoke, when Typhoo Tea was one of the good things in life.

Top right:
Mainwaring Bros sold out to PMT in 1951. This Guy Arab photographed in Longton bus station was new in 1947 with a Saunders body. In 1954 it had been fitted with a 1949 Weymann body displaced from an OPD2/1 Titan which was rebodied. Note the kiln in the background and the time clock beside the bus shelter.

Centre right:
Also taken over in 1951 was Stoke-on-Trent Motors with a mixed fleet including this Guy Arab/Duple parked outside the Stoke garage. A 1952 Burlingham-bodied Leyland Royal Tiger stands behind.

Right:
The varied Stoke-on-Trent Motors fleet was also the source of several AEC Regals including this Lawton-bodied example seen in Newcastle. The local firm of Lawton built many bodies for the independent operators in the area and must have suffered as they saw their customers being swallowed up by PMT.

Far right:
Another AEC, this time a Regal IV, came with the two-vehicle Davies Transport (Stoke) Ltd. This one had an unusual body by Metalcraft.

Above:
Baxter (Hanley) Ltd was acquired in December 1958 but operated as a subsidiary for a few months before being absorbed. This Brush-bodied AEC Regent had started life in Scotland in 1942 when it had been the first Regent to join the many Regals in the SMT fleet. It did not last long with PMT; it was sold in 1960.

Below left:
This all-Leyland PD1 had come to Baxter from Silcox of Pembroke Dock. PMT sold it to Scottish operator Clyde Coast Services.

Below:
Some of Baxter's fleet had been new to them and included this AEC Reliance/Burlingham, photographed in Stoke.

Faversham in 1961

David J. Bubier *was a bus conductor in Kent. He recalls his experiences with Maidstone & District.*

The town of Faversham, Kent, could have been said to epitomise a border point between two of the old 'territorial agreement' companies. Both East Kent and Maidstone & District maintained a small depot there and the manner in which the services radiated were to strictly defined lines. That anyone desirous of travelling by bus from, say, Canterbury to Sittingbourne would have to change at Faversham was accepted as the absolute norm with no one pausing to wonder why there was not a through service.

The town itself was of medium size and could not be described as unduly attractive although as an ancient borough it had historical pretensions as the burial place of a lesser medieval King (Stephen) and for its fisherfolk having apprehended another (James II) as that unhappy

Below:
Beadle-bodied saloon SO224 spent the greater part of its career at Preston Street depot before being preserved following a period as a farm vehicle. It is seen posed for an official view on delivery in 1957. *M&D and EK Bus Club*

monarch fled the 1688 revolution. Serving as a local centre for a sizeable area of the Garden of England it had as its principal industry brewing and the packaging of fruit and local produce.

The Maidstone & District presence in the town was as the more senior partner with a number of rural routes penetrating into the North Downs to the southwest of the town and inter-town services to Ashford and Gravesend. The town was compact and not conducive to town services but nonetheless a couple of short routes could be said to fall within this category. The centre of bus operations was the wide expanse of Court Street, reached through a narrow town centre cross-roads controlled by traffic lights, although a short relief road built with bus movements particularly in mind had eased the situation.

In 1960/61, the period with which this account is concerned, the pace of conversion of routes to one-man operation was beginning to be felt with its knock-on effects on both vehicles and staff. It was at this juncture that the writer spent an all-too-brief period working as a conductor with M&D at Faversham, an interlude in a somewhat nomadic bus career that even after 30 years can be recalled with clarity, perhaps because it was a happy and interesting time spent in the company of a small staff of excellent busmen of an old school that has all but disappeared.

During the summer of 1960 I had spent my first year as a seasonal employee with East Kent in my home town of Herne Bay. Too junior to be offered

a winter posting at nearby Canterbury it fell to my lot to be given the chance of Ashford instead. It proved difficult in that highly industrialised town to obtain any suitable digs and, having no transport, recourse was made to complex swops of duties to enable me to attend work. I would cycle to Sturry and catch a train, sometimes working alternate late/early shifts with a few hours on the upper deck of a lowbridge Guy between times.

The strain felt during that exceptionally wet autumn was great and as Christmas approached it was clear that the depot administration were equally concerned at what was going on for I often missed my day's work. One of my routes home was to take the M&D bus to Faversham, thence the train, explaining during the course of the journey my plight to the driver. A few days later he sought me out in the Mandek Social Club attached to Ashford depot and told me of a vacancy at Faversham brought about by a conductor having been trained for driving. I took the next day off and made my way to Sittingbourne to see the District Superintendent and it was arranged for me to start at Preston Street immediately after Christmas.

My arrival at M&D Faversham coincided with a number of changes in the vehicles allocated to the depot that were a prelude to what was to come.

Below:
SO215 joined the strength at Faversham at the same time as the writer and is depicted on the stand in Court Street working OMO route 16. *M&D and EK Bus Club*

The last Bristol L6A had departed as had a K6A with lowbridge bodywork which had been kept for the local routes in the town. I also just missed the last of the pre-war Leylands rebuilt as semi-integral coaches by Beadle but latterly used for crewed bus work by M&D. Their replacements made the depot allocation consist overwhelmingly of AEC Reliance saloons drawn from the various batches that the company had received from the mid-1950s on. SO215 (XKT 992) was newly arrived from Maidstone and was a Weymann-bodied example of 1957 whereas SO224 (YKR 224) had Beadle bodywork, later distinguishing itself by becoming a preserved vehicle. SO240/1/58 (240/1/58 BKM) had 1958 Harrington bodies which were far superior in design and interior layout to the others; SO240/1 had arrived together with SO285 from the shake-up at Tunbridge Wells following the opening of Tonbridge depot. SO285 was one of the latest batch of Weymann-bodied dual-purpose saloons.

Faversham required an allocation of three coaches as it was responsible for the operation of an express service daily to London (E5) although it was common M&D practice to use their coaches on crew buswork. CO425/6 (425/6 LKE) had been delivered new to the depot only a few months previously and had the Harrington Wayfarer style of body much favoured by M&D whilst the back-up was an older, central entrance model of 1954, CO312 (TKM 312). It should be mentioned that the 'O' in the fleet number stood for 'Oil engined'

and was an anachronism which was officially abandoned later in 1961. The two double-deck vehicles at Faversham (no spare was carried) were DH420/8 (RKP 901/9) these being 1953 vintage Leyland PD2/12 with Weymann Orion bodywork equipped with platform doors. During my time at Faversham we seemed to suffer a perpetual shortage of rolling stock that led to some interesting loans being made by other depots.

Kitted out with uniform trousers, summer dust jackets and a raincoat (tunics and overcoat were withheld until six months' service had been completed!) I presented myself for work at Faversham. The then relatively new, frequent electric trains enabled me to get to and from home for any shift on the rota and the depot was conveniently situated only a few yards from the station, as was my own home at the other end. The frontage of the depot included a rest room, complete with full-size snooker table, as well as the customary admin office etc. Most reliefs were effected at Court Street where an enquiry office was shared with East Kent, this dealing with our wages as well as paying in. The depot was controlled by two uniformed inspectors under the auspices of the Sittingbourne Area

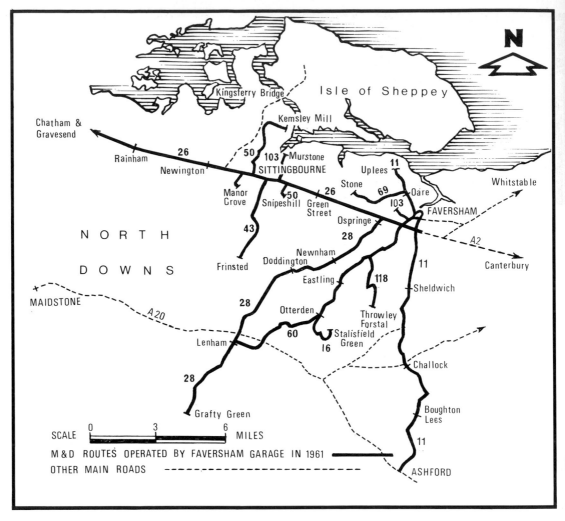

Above:
Routes operated by Faversham depot of Maidstone & District in 1961, and Sittingbourne local services worked by Faversham-based crews.

Superintendent. Following two days accompanying another conductor I was deemed fit to take my place on the staff roster. Although already an experienced conductor there were many differences in practice between East Kent and M&D, in particular the method of inserting return tickets into the machine and the issue of a 'no value' ticket to cancel. Also I was surprised to be given my own personal Setright Speed; with one of those quirks of memory I still recollect that this was number S97.

The backbone of crew work at Faversham was our contribution of two workings on the 26, a four-hour round trip to Gravesend via Chatham. Prior to the London Passenger Transport Board rationalisation of 1933 this had extended as far as Dartford and was one of the original routes of the company. In 1961 the frequency stood at 15 minutes but with only alternate journeys proceeding beyond Sittingbourne to Faversham.

Following the main A2 through Sittingbourne and Rainham the service forked off at Jezreels to Gillingham, thence via Chatham and Strood and the main road (A226) through Gadshill to Gravesend. Throughout it was a very busy route with people on and off in every section although a surprising number were on board for the full journey.

The Faversham workings were the first two 'up' in the morning at 6.30 and 7.03 with the corresponding 10.30/11.0am, 2.30/3.0pm and 6.30/7.0pm. The last bus in was, therefore, arriving back at Faversham at 11.0pm. Each of the eight journeys we worked from Faversham seemed to have its own particular characteristics or problems. The A2 was then carrying all London

Above:
The interior of Bristol L6A SO63 showing the standee layout with two-and-one seating that was very difficult for a conductor to work. *M. Coull*

to Dover traffic and congestion in the Medway towns could be severe as everything funnelled across the one road bridge available; we of course hit the rush hour at both ends of the day. It required quickness on the bell and smart fare collection by a conductor to ensure the bus ran to time, but all things considered we seemed to do fairly well. Going up, a bit of time could be made up on the last stretch into Gravesend, provided the local service had tired of waiting for you to pass and pick up his load and, late or not, we always managed to snatch a quick cup of tea at

the depot canteen there. Gravesend depot at that time had new Leyland Atlanteans and the entire batch of integral Commer TS3/Harrington saloons which found the flat roads out to the Isle of Grain to their taste.

Generally we performed the one round trip to Gravesend each day and filled in either before or after with sundry work on the local services and such journeys on the otherwise OMO routes that remained. It took only six minutes each way to run out to Bensted House Hospital on service 103, which comprised five journeys per day geared as much as anything to staff requirements. Effectively this interworked with the outer end of the 11, Ashford-Faversham, which nominally extended to Oare and Uplees but which was in practice run as a separate service. Most of the day, including evening, there was an approximately hourly service via Davington to Oare, a journey occupying seven minutes each way. This gave a glimpse of the maritime side of Faversham, The Creek, as Oare was once a thriving sailing barge centre and stood on the road down to where a ferry once plied across to the Isle of Sheppey. A further five minutes beyond took the bus to Uplees, morning and afternoon peak plus a late Saturday evening, the site of a

Below:
An all-Leyland PD2/12 about to leave Court Street for the two-hour journey to Gravesend. 26A was a route variation between Rainham and Gillingham introduced a few months after the events related in this article. *D. J. Bubier*

Above:
One of Faversham's Harrington-bodied saloons waits on the Court Street stand having arrived with a local journey from Oare on service 11. *D. J. Bubier*

former gunpowder works which (as was told me) blew up spectacularly during the Great War. The turning places at Uplees was difficult, in fact considered impossible for an OMO driver without assistance, but more of that later.

The main part of the service 11 between Faversham and Ashford ran hourly and was OMO, shared with the depot at Ashford. They also ran short workings as far as Kennington with double-decks. Certain journeys, especially on Saturday were considered too busy and thus justified putting a conductor on. It was a route most decidedly in two parts, the point where it crossed the Charing-Canterbury road at Challock determining in which direction the passengers went, there was little through traffic. On one Saturday whilst I was at Faversham the apparently not too uncommon practice was made of having a double-deck on loan from Ashford, in this instance because they borrowed one of our coaches which had been changed over on an early journey. To my delight this was one of the Daimler CWA6 (rebodied) DH49 (HKE 285) and although I was not scheduled to work any of the Ashford journeys it was on; it was possible to hi-jack it for a trip to Oare for what was my first working experience on the genre.

Three of the rural services shared a common route out of Faversham as far as Painters Forstal, where two ascended Dark Hill to serve the sizeable village of Eastling, the 16 then continuing on to Stalisfield Green some two-and-a-half miles short of Charing. This was entirely OMO and one of only two termini which I failed to reach during my career with M&D. Nominally the 16 interworked with the 60 which was the senior

route having commenced running as far as Eastling during the early 1920s. However, most of the Tuesday and Saturday journeys (two each way) were in fact crewed at this time although memory fails as to whether this was scheduled or because no OMO vehicle or driver was available. Beyond Eastling the route turned off at Corner House through some thinly populated country to eventually descend the escarpment of the North Downs to terminate in the village square of Lenham. The drivers told some dire tales of severe weather conditions that had affected this run in the past (indeed there was to be more two years later) including one where, having been forced to abandon his bus in the snow, the driver and his conductor walked the nine miles home to the depot carrying bag and punch. Both being pipe smokers they were noted to have these turned up-side down to keep out the still falling flakes of snow! Twice I worked this route, once with SO285 but the other time with another loaned vehicle, one of the final batch of Beadle rebuilds of older chassis, in this case an AEC Regal III. CO354-376 (WKM 354-76) were modelled to resemble the Harrington bodies on contemporary Reliance chassis and were not unattractive vehicles. Unlike other Beadle rebuilds they did not have a bulkhead between the driver and passengers. They were always amongst my favourites and I was sorry one was never preserved.

Whilst at Lenham on the afternoon working of the 60 one met up with the outer end of the other

North Downs route from Faversham. This was the 28 which on four days of the week provided five journeys out to Newnham and Doddington, villages that were also served by a separate service from Sittingbourne rather more frequently. Tuesdays and Saturdays saw journeys extended, like the 60, through isolated small hamlets to Lenham and then beyond to Grafty Green. Presumably there must have been some traffic justification for this but one wonders whether many 2s4d (12p) tickets were ever issued for the through journey. The 28 was also a full OMO route, so I never got to Grafty Green, but school journeys to Doddington morning and afternoon were crew-operated. These particular children were the bane of my life and played me up considerably, sensing as they always do someone who was not going to keep perfect discipline. In fact it was several more years before I learnt that knack and I envied teachers and other busmen who managed it so easily!

Mention has been made of a third route that shared a common road as far as Painters Forstal with the Eastling services. This was the 118 and was different in that it was entirely a crewed operation comprising three Wednesday and five Saturday journeys to Throwley Forstal, the lanes traversed being parallel to and about one mile distant from the main Faversham-Ashford road. It certainly carried substantial loads and I was told had been known to have the double-deck sent out in the past.

My sense of propriety was almost immediately outraged when I discovered that several of the passengers were conveying battery accumulators, an item specifically prohibited by the rule book.

Below:
SO215 was the oldest of the single-deckers allocated to Faversham and had Weymann bodywork. It is about to depart for Ashford. *D. J. Bubier*

With great patience the driver explained that there were still a number of homes out there without mains electric and that the batteries for their wirelesses had to be taken into town and exchanged for recharged ones. I retired defeated, once more finding that the rule book was subject to the all-embracing hand of expediency and old Chinese customs! The village of Throwley Forstal, devoid of public transport, is today the province of the luxury weekend second-home set, a very far cry from that period only 30 years ago, and little changed in 50 before that, where virtually the entire village boarded the weekly bus into town.

The Throwley Forstal service interworked on Saturday with the 69, another curiosity that one was forced to ponder the origins or purpose of. This followed the route of the service 11 to Oare and then turned left and proceeded in the general direction of Teynham for nine minutes to what was, in the timetable, termed Stone but amounted to no more than a level crossing and a farm. We picked up few passengers other than between Oare and town. Even the long-time staff were a little bemused by the 69 but it soldiered on for quite some years before it occurred to someone to axe it.

As time slipped by into the spring of that year I found myself adapting to the routine of work at Preston Street quite easily. The shifts were quite tolerable even if I was away from home for long periods, six days a week. We did not have much Sunday work, still two on the 26, the morning ones only going to Chatham and generally a saloon was used. Both the OMO Ashford and Stalisfield Green routes had Sunday journeys. There was plenty of free time between journeys once the daily round to Gravesend was completed in which to adjourn to the cafe hard by the enquiry office to play the juke box or maybe to be instructed in the finer points of snooker at the depot by one of the drivers.

Without exception they were a good crowd of mates to work with and tolerant to a callow youth. I learnt a lot during that period. Our local passengers I soon got to know and (with the possible exception of the Doddington schoolchildren) came to like a great deal. The 26 was a route that was never boring to work on. I began to think in terms of permanence and even of actually moving to Faversham in order to develop my off-duty social life in the town as well. However, talk increasingly came around to the question of the second phase of OMO conversion which would take in the remainder of the crew work other than the 26 and how this was to be accomplished. The very tight turning place at Uplees became the talking point but was eventually dismissed by the company after the depot maintenance foreman performed the feat, in daylight, unassisted by observing head office staff and trade union representatives. Having myself watched drivers back from inside the rear of a saloon during evening gloom and rain I was not sure whether any worthwhile guidance was possible since I couldn't see anything out there anyway!

For one week the depot played host to its first Leyland Atlantean when one, DH564 (564 LKP), arrived for trials with the Loadmeter with which it was fitted. This was my first experience of the modern rear-engined double-deck and I found it eerie one night to stand by the driver as we drove through thick fog up the A2. The drivers differed in their opinions, bearing in mind none had received any prior training on the type, but most thought they represented a change for the better. Ominously one said the day would come when he would be expected to operate it one-man. Passengers already knew the type from when the other depots used them on the 26, in fact the variety of types being employed on the full service was considerable ranging from vintage Bristols to this modernistic concept. When the time came for the Atlantean to return, Gillingham played a dirty trick and sent down about the oldest Bristol they could find, in fact one due for imminent withdrawal. It was so rough to ride on at the back that it made a round trip to Gravesend something of an ordeal and we all complained for a week. Finally I popped my head around the corner of the depot one morning, saw what was on the 7.03am 'up' and promptly went back home, reporting in sick later. No comment was made subsequently about this piece of indiscipline but the loss of a day's pay was worth it: the Bristol disappeared that very day and our beloved PD2 was returned!

We had a Leyland-bodied PD2 for a short while following an accident at Strood when a lorry took several lower deck windows out of DH428. After transferring our passengers we went back to Gillingham where, to my astonishment, we at first were given an ex-Chatham & District Guy Arab that was on the forecourt. The type was rare at Gillingham, being normally at Luton depot and seldom seen outside of the Medway towns. As we went back empty to Chatham to pick up our schedule for the down journey I had visions of getting this beast back to Faversham and somehow hanging on to it; I was after all an ex-East Kent man! Unfortunately someone realised the enormity of it all so when we arrived back at Gillingham 15 minutes later they had dug out a Leyland for us to change to and my experience of M&D Guys was all too brief.

The return of that Leyland to its home depot was tinged with high farce when it was arranged

Above:
DH49 put in a brief appearance at Faversham during the writer's time but is seen here on its more usual haunt, Kennington short workings of service 11. *D. J. Bubier*

that, following completion of the last bus in, my driver was to go back up with it to Gillingham where he would get a lift back with one of our coaches that was completing a private hire there at about the requisite small hours of the morning. This was in fact the driver who had recently passed his test and who I had replaced as a conductor. At the depot I got out to direct a couple of youths who should have got off on the A2 as they planned to hitch to Dover, I turned to see my bus disappear down the street with my Setright and cash bag loose on the back seat! I was so concerned with that problem that what everyone else was hopping up and down about escaped me; the bus had turned along Stone Street and was heading for Ospringe under a low bridge! A saloon was hurriedly pulled out and we went in fear of the worst, but incredibly he had managed to go under as far as we could see. All that was left was to phone ahead to Gillingham and make sure that my bag was recovered, which it was although I was quite a few shillings shown as short at the end of the week.

The discussions were over and our new duties were posted. We were to keep our own journeys on the 26 but in most instances were now to be relieved at Sittingbourne either going up or coming back. In place of our local work at Faversham we were to perform duties at Sittingbourne, this including a lot of 'stand by' time. Several split shifts were now included. They had managed to find work for us on the town service 124, quite one of the most appalling services I have ever experienced. It ran from one side of Sittingbourne, (Manor Grove Estate) to a dusty hole called Murston at the other in around 12 minutes; I took an instant dislike to most of the passengers. We were also allocated some duties on service 50 running between Kemsley Paper Mill and Snipeshill and this brought me into contact with SO63. During the period when M&D had been a good customer of Bristol they had taken a couple of batches of very Tilling-like L6As with Eastern Coach Works rear entrance bodywork. A couple of these had been later converted to standee layout (30 seats plus 30 standees); SO63 (MKN 212) was the survivor and was to be withdrawn later that year.

Below:
Atlantean DH564 seen during its stay at Faversham during Loadmeter trials early in 1961, rounding the top of Preston Street on service 26. *D. J. Bubier*

The perversity of officialdom decreed that SO63 had the capacity of a double-deck and was, perforce, to be used as one. We arrived at Kemsley Mill in good time and stood outside the bus as seemingly hundreds of workers poured out and tried to board the single-deck Bristol. In disbelief I had to turn several off in order to be able myself to get inside and there was no possibility of collecting fares other than as the workers got off. The next day we had a conventional double-deck which was somewhat easier but, lo, there was SO63 for the same ritual the following day! We gained the impression that the Sittingbourne men shunned this vehicle and that the garage saw in us Faversham crews a good chance to let it get some mileage in. It was even given to us to perform the wholly incongruous task of duplicating a journey on service 43 to Frinstead. This was then worked OMO by one of the Harrington-bodied Albion Nimbus small capacity saloons which was clearly not large enough for the busier market days.

During the periods of enforced idleness that I had now to spend at Sittingbourne the place to be found was a coffee bar known as The Boomerang. Here I played on the juke box the latest records by Cliff Richard and Elvis Presley. Briefly I started to date a local girl but the relationship was doomed by the necessary to and froing involved between Herne Bay and Sittingbourne. Even single it was clear that far too great a proportion of my wages were being taken up by all the initial travelling to Faversham and then spending on snacks, etc, during working time. The duties were now long and to me no longer as interesting as they had been at first and I was far from happy. It was almost inevitable that I accepted an offer to return to East Kent at Herne Bay at the beginning of May. In all I had worked from Faversham for M&D for a mere four months although it had seemed much longer.

Faversham was to see very great changes over the ensuing years. Rationalisation brought about the eventual closure of the East Kent garage and for a while both companies worked out of Preston Street before that too was closed. The creation of the National Bus Company meant the end of the traditional boundary and M&D green reached Whitstable and through services ran between Canterbury, Sittingbourne and Maidstone. The former rural routes are now all gone except the 16 to Stalisfield which went over to independent operation with the closure of the depot whilst the tendering process has put another operator on the erstwhile 11.

The assistance of the records of the M&D and EK Bus Club is acknowledged for that information which failing memories failed to call to mind.

Eastern Counties

The Eastern Counties Omnibus Company once served much of East Anglia. **Geoff Mills** *illustrates how it has changed.*

The Eastern Counties Omnibus Co was formed in 1931 to combine four existing operators in East Anglia, in an area which included the major centres of Cambridge, Great Yarmouth, Ipswich, Norwich and Peterborough.

In 1984 the western part of the company was reformed as Cambus, with its headquarters in Cambridge. Cambus was privatised in a management buy-out from the National Bus Company in December 1986; Eastern Counties was sold by NBC to its management in February 1987. In September 1989 Cambus was split into two, with its Peterborough-based operations being taken over by Viscount Bus & Coach, a wholly-owned Cambus subsidiary.

Below left:
Surrey Street bus station, Norwich, was the heart of Eastern Counties' territory in 1963. This Leyland Titan PPD1A, nearing the end of its life, was new in 1947 and had 53-seat Eastern Coach Works lowbridge bodywork.

Below:
In 1970 this 1952 Bristol KSW with 60-seat ECW bodywork could be found on city services in Cambridge. The Eastern Counties operating territory was flat, and this was a KSW5G with 94bhp five-cylinder Gardner engine, deemed powerful enough for the untaxing terrain. It was withdrawn a few months after this photograph was taken in the railway yard at Cambridge.

Above:
Peterborough in 1962, with an Eastern Counties Bristol L5G loaded for a trip to March. New in 1950 it had an ECW coach body which had been downgraded for bus operation in 1957. The use of rear entrances for single-deckers was dying out when this bus was delivered.

Left:
Cambridge still has a bus station in Drummer Street, where this Bristol MW5G with Gardner's horizontal 5HLW five-cylinder 6.97-litre engine was photographed in April 1965 on its first week in service. The ECW body had 45 seats and at this time the bus was crew-operated.

Below:
Ipswich is still served by Eastern Counties, but not with Bristol REs. Ten ECW-bodied RELL6G dual-purpose machines were delivered in 1970, one of which is seen in June that year leaving Ipswich for Colchester. It is one-man operated.

Above:
This rare machine, operating in Norwich with the helpful destination 'Service', a common Eastern Counties practice, was an ECW-bodied Bedford VAM, one of four in the fleet. It ran from 1967 to 1976.

Below:
Under NBC control the Eastern Counties livery changed from Tilling red to NBC's corporate poppy red with the standard NBC style fleetname and logo. This 1962 Bristol Lodekka FLF6G was new to Lincolnshire Road Car and is seen in Peterborough soon after acquisition by Eastern Counties in 1973. It survived until 1983.

Above:
In the run-up to privatisation NBC's corporate grip relaxed and this Bristol VRT appeared in a short-lived red, black and yellow livery – but still with NBC-style fleetname. It is seen in Norwich bus station in August 1986.

Below:
The privatised Eastern Counties company adopted a deep red livery with cream and orange stripes, as worn by this 1979 Mark 1 Leyland National which the company converted to Gardner 6HLX power in 1981 because of dissatisfaction with the Leyland 510 engine. The radiator was relocated from the rear to the front, initially under a protruding grille but later behind this National 2 front end assembly.

Above left:
A reversed, predominantly cream, livery was used by Eastern Counties for two Leyland Olympian double-deck coaches delivered in 1989 – the company's first new double-deckers since 1981. The Olympians had Gardner 6LXB engines and Northern Counties lowheight bodies.

Left:
Cambus adopted a pale blue livery, as worn by this 1974 Bristol RELH6G which was part of the initial Cambus fleet when the company was separated from Eastern Counties. It has a 49-seat ECW body and is on the company's Eastline service to Ipswich.

Above:
The insipid pale blue was replaced by an attractive combination of two-tone blue and cream. This far-travelled ECW-bodied Bristol VRT was new in 1976 to PMT and arrived at Cambus in 1986 by way of North Devon Red Bus. Above the main Cambus fleetname it carries the legend 'Cambridge & District'.

Centre right:
This Leyland Royal Tiger Doyen was in the fleet from 1987 to 1989, operating in National Express livery. It is seen in December 1987 leaving Cambridge for Ipswich on the same service as the Bristol RE illustrated opposite but offering considerably more comfort. Did RE passengers pay less?

Right:
The first full-size saloon to receive Viscount's yellow, white and blue livery was this 1981 Leyland National which had originally operated for Eastern Counties and then for Cambus. It is seen at Peterborough bus station in September 1989.

The Green Line riddle

London's Green Line coach network has undergone many changes. **John Aldridge** *examines the operation's changing face.*

As this book is an annual, by rights you should perhaps be reading this article after Christmas dinner, or maybe on Boxing Day.

If that is so, I can offer you a riddle every bit as ridiculous, inconsequential or unanswerable as those found in Christmas crackers: when is a Green Line not a Green Line?

Acceptable answers could be when it is a bus, or when it is on a route not numbered in the 700s, or when it is not green, or when it is operated by Luton & District.

Let us take a step or two backwards, in fact let us step back almost 62 years to the start of Green Line Coaches. The original concept was a regular service of comfortable buses running on a limited-stop basis from outer London into central London.

Most of the time the vehicles were above average. Compared to the single-deck London bus

Below:
Changes: a new Park Royal-bodied AEC Reliance (right) stands with an RF and a long Routemaster coach outside the now closed Windsor garage in 1972.

Top:

Light and airy: looking rearwards inside an Alexander-bodied AEC Swift. There were only four inward-facing seats, at the front nearside.

Centre:

Not special: the second batch of Leyland Nationals were 10.3m long and had seats trimmed in moquette, but were just buses.

Above:

New image: Duple-bodied AEC Reliance (left) and a Duple-bodied Leyland Leopard, both lettered for the Heathrow-Gatwick Jetlink 747 service, stand at Staines garage.

of the day, they generally boasted luggage racks, heaters, doors and better upholstered seats. Some purists used to argue that they were not coaches because proper coaches were more than tarted-up buses.

But except perhaps on summer Sundays or special occasions or rush hours, a proper Green Line offered more comfort than a bus. Its crews used to be more senior and better paid than their country bus colleagues working from the same garages.

Green Line services were suspended, resumed, and then suspended again in the Second World War, and did not reappear until 1946. This gives rise to a bit of inaccuracy in subsequent celebrations. Green Line marked its 50th anniversary with a rally and appropriate junketings in 1980. Three different books were published to mark the event.

The appropriate junketings in 1990 were rather more muted and produced no books. Yet probably more happened to Green Line between 1980 and 1990 than in any previous decade.

The inaccuracy is that no account has been taken of time off the road between late 1942 and early 1946. The company, in one form or another, might have been going all those years, but the services certainly weren't. The year 1993 might be a more appropriate time to celebrate Green Line's 60th anniversary.

But I digress. When Green Line was re-established in 1946, the routes were numbered in the 700s, and most operated across London: for example, Windsor-London-Sevenoaks. That was not because there was much potential for through traffic but because it made operational sense.

Working shifts were quite attractive to crews too, with one out and return journey and a couple of other bits representing a full shift. Thus an early shift Staines crew on the 701 Ascot-Staines-London-Gravesend service might start with the 07.08 Staines garage to Ascot (arr 07.33), 07.38 Ascot to Gravesend (arr 10.27), run empty to nearby Northfleet garage, have almost an hour's meal relief, then work the 11.38 Gravesend to Ascot (arr 14.26), leave Ascot 14.38, and be relieved at Staines garage at about 15.03.

In the 1960s traffic began to drift away as more people bought cars, and those cars helped to create more congestion in central London which made timekeeping less reliable, and lost more potential passengers.

Proposals for one-man operation were resisted by the unions, and resulted in a decision wherever possible to go double-deck (replacing the ageing RF coaches by Routemaster coaches). To make the necessary economies, that meant making half-hourly single-deck routes into hourly

double-deck ones, which made the services less attractive for many.

After the National Bus Company was set up and the Government handed the country bus and coach part of London Transport to it, the newly formed London Country Bus Services moved as quickly as possible to replace conductor-operated RMCs and RCLs by one-man single-deckers. The first big batch of vehicles bought, 90 AEC Reliances with Park Royal bodies, were not bad from the passengers' point of view.

The 87 Leyland Nationals that followed soon after were pretty passenger-unfriendly, but it took an outcry in the technical press and many complaints from passengers before NBC ungraciously conceded the point, and 87 more Nationals that followed had coach-type seats, overhead luggage racks and other comforts.

For Green Line, most of the 1970s were really a period of decline punctuated by strange interludes. One, by chance, produced the most passenger-friendly Green Lines ever built. When the NBC got going, its first acts on the engineering side were to expand as far as possible the vehicle standardisation policy of the former Tilling Group. That meant as many Bristol-ECW vehicles as could be built to be supplied to as many operators as possible. Once that programme was completed came the Atlantean and Fleetline double-deckers and, finally, the smaller vehicle batches such as AEC Swifts for South Wales Transport and East Kent.

By the time the NBC got round to those last, it found that the municipal operators had already

Above:
Moved: After industrial problems, the Luton service was lost to Luton & District. An ECW-bodied Tiger, with prominent details for the service, stands in, of all places, Brighton.

placed their orders for both chassis and bodywork, and it was hard to find a willing bodybuilder for a relatively modest number of Swifts. However, an order went to Alexander and included 21 for South Wales Transport.

As the building date neared, South Wales Transport was not doing too well financially, so it

Below:
Changed colours: a former Duple-bodied Tiger of Green Line, now in Luton & District's red and grey, leaves Victoria for Stevenage.

was decided to divert the vehicles to LCBS for use as Green Lines. At a relatively late stage Alexander revamped the interior of its W bus body design to something nearer a coach.

The resulting vehicles might not have been the driver's ideal, as they were a bit underpowered. But they were probably the passenger's ideal. A gently ramped floor gave excellent forward visibility from all seats – far better than on many proper coaches – and deep and long side windows aided side visibility and gave a light and airy interior.

Another strange interlude, on the debit side, occurred on one of the shorter routes running into Aldgate. Long after conversion to one-man single-deckers, a crew-operated Routemaster was a not infrequent performer. Staff shortages meant that sometimes the only driver available was a relatively new one who had not yet done his one-man training, so a Routemaster, complete with conductor, would be used.

Vehicle shortages, staff shortages, maintenance problems, and the three-day week all contributed to the trials of the 1970s.

But a turning point came in 1977 when the first of 60 AEC Reliance coaches – proper high-class coaches – started to arrive on a five-year lease from dealer Kirkby Central. At the same time Green Line moved away, some would say inevitably, from cross-London operations, of which the last ran in 1979, and began building up other useful services, for example to London's airports, which had been rather neglected by the network.

Within a few years, Green Line had also joined the National Express network, had expanded private hire activities under the Green Line name, and had begun a kind of feeder service to Walthamstow to connect with the Victoria Line tube, rather like the original first Green Line route to Golders Green.

Because the old restricted area of operation no longer applied, it was able to reach valuable destinations such as Oxford or Cambridge jointly with fellow NBC operators.

Deregulation of express services permitted the introduction of commuter services, whose success was partly helped by the failings of and high fares on British Rail. More recently we have seen deregulation of bus services outside London, and later the division of LCBS into four companies and their subsequent privatisation.

County councils are now inevitably involved with loss-making services and Green Line routes have been no exception. But county councils are naturally not interested in Green Line networks or history: their remit is merely to devise suitable services to be run at minimum cost to serve the needs of localities that might otherwise be left unserved.

Some uneconomic routes have thus vanished. Others have come to be operated by other

Top:

Bus substitute: not long after Sovereign took over Jubilee Coaches, one of the latter's Leyland Lynx buses stands at Victoria, having brought in a load of commuters.

Above:

Another name: a London Express-liveried Tiger Plaxton of London Country North West is on one of the more frequent Green Line routes, to Hemel Hempstead.

concerns: thus my riddle, when is a Green Line not a Green Line? Does a coach in Armchair's orange and white livery, bearing route number 733 and sitting in Watford bus station en route to Heathrow, still count as a Green Line, at least in spirit?

Another strange case is the Guildford to London Green Line, 715. After it was diverted to serve

Kingston en route, a rush hours-only variant was introduced for commuters, which followed the old route and bypassed Kingston. More recently, it came to be operated by Blue Saloon of Guildford, and numbered 510. But the last Surrey County Council timetable I have seen shows it back with London Country South West (fleetname London & Country), still as route 510, still limited stop, but no longer called a Green Line. But I bet that the same coaches work 510 as 715.

When LCBS was split into four separate companies, they agreed to keep the joint Green Line operation and livery. The four companies were London Country North West, LC South West, LC North East and LC South East. North West has kept its name, South West now calls itself London & Country, and South East was soon renamed Kentish Bus & Coach. North East subsequently split into Sovereign Bus & Coach and County Bus & Coach. Later than that Sovereign acquired the Stevenage operations of Jubilee Travel, and then in May 1990 most of Sovereign was taken over by Luton & District. Down south, London & Country moved its airport services into a separate company, Speedlink Airport Services, though the Luton-Heathrow-Gatwick service 747 is still operated jointly with two of the others.

Despite the intention on livery, a visit today at rush hour to London's Eccleston Bridge and Buckingham Palace Road terminals at Victoria can be a colourful business. You can see plenty of green Green Lines. You are likely to see other colours too, and sometimes other names, such as Kentish Coach or even (on a Kentish Coach) Shearings National. Then there are a few Green Lines painted instead in a London Express livery

as part of a joint scheme to offer London suburban connections on selected timings suitable for connecting with National Express services from Victoria coach station.

Not long ago, I saw an ex-Jubilee Leyland Lynx – hardly a coach or even a semi-coach – sitting at Eccleston Bridge, having brought in a load of commuters. But the most prominent other colour is Luton & District, with red and grey, often on Duple-bodied Tigers which were originally part of a large batch bought by LCBS in 1986, just before the original fragmentation into four companies.

Recently at Sevenoaks I spotted a 705 off-peak journey being worked by a Kentish Bus Talbot Pullman: by no stretch of the imagination was that a coach. But that route has now gone over to Metrobus of Orpington, which runs it into Victoria coach station, though it is really only a commuter service.

Green Lines may often not be green any more. They may not be numbered in the 700s either. But if you look around you may still see them providing some kind of limited stop service, though you may need a knowledge of bus route and company history to make a positive identification.

Reinventing the bus

Stephen Morris *muses over the development of the minibus and concludes there's nothing new under the sun.*

As a commentator on the bus industry there is one question which I dread being asked, and as is often the way of things it is inevitably a question one does get asked frequently. That question is 'how successful has deregulation been?' It is one of the great imponderables of our time, as the answer to it depends really on where one stands. If you happen to be called Brian and come from Perth, and can remember starting a coach service with coach deregulation in 1980 and can now stand in Barrow, Burnley, Bedford, Belper, Brighton or Bognor and see buses in a white livery with orange red and blue stripes applied in the same racy fashion as one those few pioneering coaches over a decade ago, you would probably conclude that you were quietly satisfied with its effects. If you were a former Potteries bus conductor called Harry, your view might depend rather on whether you were standing in Exeter, Oxford or the Isle of Dogs at the time. If your name was J. Public Esq, it would depend on the location of the bus stop at which you did most of your standing. After deregulation, the bus stop at which I did most of my standing was served – or sometimes not – by an incredibly mixed assortment of vehicles, including Volvo B58s with Plaxton Viewmaster bodywork, a TAZ Dubrava, and sometimes an unmarked Caetano Optimo alongside less exotic hardware, and more often than not it was easier to walk or accept a lift from a passing colleague. Now all that has changed; the same bus stop is now served by red buses with funny stripes which look like London buses but call themselves Westlink. Standard fare is a little Ford Transit, it usually comes on time and

delivers me to the office five minutes before starting time, and if your experience of deregulated buses is that good, then possibly deregulation has been a success. You are also probably one of the lucky ones.

There is only one thing which can be said about deregulation with any certainty; it has brought about no end of strange happenings, such that events which prior to 1986 would have been earth-shattering news nowadays do not warrant much more than a brief item in 'News Update' in *Buses*. One of those strange happenings has been the rise of the modern minibus.

For a start, under pre-deregulation wisdom minibuses could not possibly work, other than in

Below:
Grand junketings as the Transits roll into town, in this case Weston-super-Mare, the first major conversion of an entire town network. *S. Morris*

118

a few rural locations or for welfare work, and yet somehow since deregulation became flavour of the month the old logic has been overturned. Yet the strange effects of the minibus have run deeper than that. The effect which they had on the seemingly irreversible march of technology is worthy of comment. Before World War 1 a typical bus might have a front-mounted, in-line four-cylinder engine in a bonnet sticking out in front, a manual gearbox, mechanical brakes, a width of about 7ft and a length around 20ft. By the end of the 1920s the layout would not have changed too much, but efforts would have been made to lower the floor height, the six-cylinder engine would be mounted alongside the driver, overall dimensions would have grown to 7ft 6in wide by 26ft long and vacuum brakes and pneumatic tyres would certainly be in vogue. By the time of World War 2 you might well have an epicyclic preselector gearbox and fluid flywheel to make driving easier. If you were very avant-garde you might just have air brakes. By the end of the 1950s, if you were in the vanguard of technology your buses might be of integral alloy construction, have independent coil suspension, power steering, power-hydraulic brakes and fully automatic transmission with dimensions anything up to 30ft long 8ft wide. Or you might have the engine mounted across the frame at the back, with a low, stepless platform

alongside the driver. By 1980 you would almost certainly have the six-cylinder engine at the back, out of the way, good access, air suspension, and you might even be turbocharged, with fully-automatic transmission, air brakes with spring operation of the handbrake and power steering; your driver could just press button A (or should that be button D), sit behind a nice big windscreen in his shirt sleeves in the depths of winter and point the thing effortlessly in the right direction.

Yet the new bus of 1985 would probably have a four-cylinder diesel in-line at the front, a clutch pedal, a manual gearbox, steering without any power assistance, brakes operated by the weight

Left:
As bigger vehicles came into fashion so the Dodge 50 had a new lease of life. GM Buses 1907 (D907 NDB), seen in Stockport, has Northern Counties bodywork. *J. G. Milnes*

Below left:
Another source of bigger minibuses was Iveco, whose Turbo Daily became popular with bodywork by Robin Hood. Another Greater Manchester bus is 1515 (D515 MJA), seen in Cheadle. *S. Morris*

Below:
Optare's VW-based CityPacer brought new style to minibuses. This one belonged to Leicester City Transport's Loughborough Coach & Bus subsidiary which operated as Trippit. *S. Morris*

of the driver's foot acting against hydraulic fluid, though probably with a bit of vacuum assistance, a mechanical handbrake, a bonnet sticking out of the front and a little narrow entrance with three fairly steep steps. And the overall dimensions would probably be about 7ft by 20ft. Suspension would more than likely be by steel cart springs – but at least the tyres would be pneumatic! This was the new revolutionary form of transport, the great innovation of the 1980s – yet in terms of technology it was decades behind its predecessors.

The minibus revolution predated deregulation by more than two years. It is sometimes difficult to trace the origins of a particular form of transport once it became widespread; yet with minibuses one can really be quite specific. The place was Exeter, the date was 27 February 1984. Granted, one cannot pretend that Devon General invented the minibus. Eastern Counties, for instance, had operated them in various locations during the 1970s, Crosville had had them in the 1960s. Even London Transport had had a few, and the Post Office ran lots of them. But the introduction of 16-seat Ford Transits (converted from parcel vans by Midland Red Engineering, in the same factory which was building underfloor-engined single-deckers with independent rubber suspension and full integral construction 30 years or more earlier and by 1958 was building motorway coaches capable of reaching the magic 'ton') in large quantities to replace conventional double-deckers on an urban route was something new and, though at the time it just seemed like an experiment with not too great a future few people realised just how far-reaching a development it would be in a very short time.

In fairness the Ford Transits with their regressive technology were only a part of the story. A whole package of new measures was involved, which represented a seachange in the way buses were seen. I remember arriving in Exeter on a National Express coach in 1984, not knowing anything about this great 'experiment' and seeing advertising hoardings asking 'What's red, yellow and black and won't be long?', and showing a side view of a Ford Transit with MiniBus writ large on its sides. A major advertising campaign for a humble bus service? Now that *is* radical. . . The buses themselves were certainly different. At a time when NBC poppy green, or whatever the drab shade was, reigned supreme, a big wedge-shaped band of bright yellow, black skirt and bold lettering without a hint of an NBC symbol anywhere was radical too, though we little knew then what radical things were to follow in terms of image. There are some things it is better not to know in advance.

Delving deeper into this strange phenomenon, it
transpired that frequencies were increased to the
extent that passengers no longer needed
timetables, and once outside the city centre buses
would stop almost anywhere on demand and also
opened up new sections of route. Moreover the
minibuses were part of a separate unit from the
big buses, with their own pool of drivers, recruited
specially for the job.

The Exeter experiment was actually an NBC
initiative, based on a submission by John
Hargreaves, chairman of NBC's South region,
Derek Fytche, chairman of National Products, the
coaching and leisure divisions of NBC, and Brian
Barrett, NBC's director of marketing. At the time
of their submission in August 1983 there had
already been tentative moves towards minibus
operation on a large scale by the private sector,
with Lunar Module in Luton having already
gained the go-ahead for its scheme, and a Mr
Tony Shephard pressing on towards a proposed
large-scale minibus operation in London, called
AMOS. Thus NBC had been alerted to the
potential of minibus operation after deregulation
and was recognising the importance of leading the
field, in order to protect the interests of its
subsidiary companies, rather than having to
institute a rearguard action at a later date. Exeter
was chosen for a number of reasons, not least

that the local services there did not receive
revenue support and so NBC could do almost
what it liked with them, it was fairly typical of
towns served by NBC and the local trade unions
were amenable to the scheme. It was proposed
that NBC should meet the capital costs involved
and make up any additional costs incurred by
minibus operation in Exeter.

It was soon found that the minibus experiment
was surprisingly successful. The new image
surrounding the new buses, the improved
frequencies, the hail-and-ride aspects and the
improved penetration all had the desired effect
and passenger increases were substantial, not
least amongst car owners. Costs were kept down
in a number of ways; the purchase price of the
minibuses was obviously low, the drivers had
been employed on lower rates than 'conventional'
bus drivers and there were no premiums for
overtime. Also the buses themselves helped in
reducing costs; mechanical units could be
replaced, rather than repaired, quite cheaply
without the same skill levels being necessary. It
was quoted at the time that a Transit engine could
be replaced for the same price as replacing a

Leyland National alternator. Moreover, despite the doubts of the sceptics (including the author!) the Transit proved to be a remarkably durable and rugged vehicle in the cut and thrust of urban bus operation.

The idea spread like wildfire in the following months leading up to deregulation, though it was perhaps noticeable that many of the initial conversions to minibus operation were in Mr Hargreaves' South region. During the first half of 1985, there were a number of smallish schemes introduced, notably in Witney and Abingdon by South Midland, which had operated minibuses in Jericho for a year or two prior to that, Midland Red (North) in Stafford and Southern Vectis in Ryde and Cowes. However the next stage was the conversion of an entire town network at Weston-super-Mare, where Badgerline replaced 18 buses with 46 Minilink Ford Transits on high frequency services, using 80 drivers. It was launched in a blaze of glory by Ernie Wise on 31 May 1985. By the end of the year Midland Fox had introduced 100 minibuses into Leicester and Midland Red West had converted its entire Worcester city operation, using 61 vehicles. What was interesting about Worcester though was its choice of vehicle; most schemes so far had used Ford Transit 16-seaters, though Oxford for one had found you could just about get away with 20 seats on the biggest Transit chassis cab option (in actual fact once standees were taken into account the 16-seater had a bigger passenger capacity, and in both cases a full load put you very close to the vehicle's design gross vehicle weight). However in Worcester the size was increased slightly, using the Mercedes-Benz L608D van as a base. This was a bit narrower than the Transit, so single seats only could be fitted on one side, which had beneficial effects in giving wider seats and gangways than on the rather cramped Transits, but even so 20 seats could be fitted with ease.

Probably the major factor in vehicle choice was what was available. Ford was developing a new Transit so was delighted to have a ready market for the remaining production of the old. Similarly the Mercedes L608D was coming to the end of the road, and again NBC was an ideal dumping ground to clear the stocks for the new model. In both cases however the van market was the greatest priority to the manufacturers, so no suitable version of the new Transit or Mercedes was available from the launch of the new model

and the gap had to be plugged with other things. NBC bought hundreds of Freight Rover Sherpas, as did one of the few major new independents, United Transport Buses, which set up in Manchester in a big way as Manchester Minibuses, alias the Bee Line Buzz Co, after deregulation in January 1987. Opinions were divided on the quality of the Sherpas; some operators seemed to manage to make them work, but within the NBC camp it was perceived as less reliable than the trusty Transit, and Sherpas were

Above:

Transit Holdings developed its own curious style of bodywork for 16-seat Ford Transits, built by Mellor. It looked a bit ungainly but was actually very practical and more 'user-friendly' than most. No 223 (E223 BDV) was one of them used by Docklands Transit in East London.
S. Morris

Below:

Optare's answer for the 30-seat market was the StarRider, based on the Mercedes-Benz 811D London Buses took a variety of larger minibuses, including StarRider SR66. It opted for a reduced seating capacity with full-width entrance and improved circulation. *R. J. Waterhouse*

pushed around from pillar to post before they landed with an operator prepared to take them, and when replacements became due often newer Sherpas were chopped rather than early Transits.

There was no doubt that minibuses were achieving their objectives of getting more people on buses and cutting costs. Frequencies, hail and ride, effective marketing, an image as something new and more fun than conventional buses, with friendly drivers all had their effect, and as NBC – and others – got caught up in the excitement there was little time to stop and take stock of the situation. By the end of 1985 there were 500 in service with NBC and this figure had risen to nearly 4,000 by the time of deregulation in October 1986.

The basic concept was obviously successful, but there were detailed problems. The parcel-van vehicles were undoubtedly a compromise; there was an amazing discovery that the shoppers the services had set out to woo came back with shopping, which was a bit of a nuisance as there was nowhere to put it. Internally, it has to be said, most minibus convertors did a good job of making quite a plush environment; externally there was no getting away from the fact that the minibuses were based fairly and squarely on delivery vans (the writer once hailed a yellow Transit pick-up truck in Leicester, thinking it to be a Midland Fox Cub!). Also lacking was adequate ventilation, the driver's position was usually too low, and as minibuses proved a success in generating traffic then their capacity proved just too small. What was really needed was something bigger, and better still something purpose built. . .

Something bigger was not too difficult to produce. This just involved getting slightly bigger van bases, and these were available from Dodge and Iveco. The Dodge 50-series was, not wishing to be unkind, rather antedeluvian. It had its origins in the old Commer Walkthru van, had been sold as a Karrier, then a Dodge, and before long was to become a Renault, perhaps rather unfortunately giving the impression of a lack of patriotism to passengers who could be forgiven for not realising that their Renaults were built nowhere more Gallic than Dunstable. It was a rather rough and ready vehicle, with poor suspension, but it was readily available and could accommodate 25 seats. The Iveco product was foreign, built by Fiat, the Turbo Daily 49.10 and this too, when combined with a proper coach-built body could provide seats for 25. Both caught on in a big way, though in general the Dodge/Renaults went to operators with a municipal background, which seemed faintly appropriate somehow. Greater Manchester Buses bought them in droves to try to see off the UTB Sherpas. This phase of minibus development brought in some of the traditional big bus bodybuilders to a greater extent. Only Alexander had really got into parcel van conversion, but it was joined by Northern Counties and East Lancs in this new wave.

Two other players in the 25-seat field had slightly different ideas. MCW and Optare both saw the desire for 25-seaters and both also grasped the nettle of producing something custom-built and which would present a more stylish exterior. First in was Optare, which teamed up with

Below:
Bournemouth tried second-hand Sherpas for a while, and then needed something bigger. It took a batch of Wadham Stringer-bodied Mercedes-Benz 811D 31-seaters, but got rid of them with almost indecent haste in favour of double-deckers. No 48 (F48 XPR) is seen in The Square. *K. Lane*

Volkswagen to produce the very stylish CityPacer. This brought added sophistication; the vehicle looked as if it had been designed for the job rather than knocked together from an existing van; moreover the styling was even more up to date than anything offered in the way of big buses. Additional sophistication came from the use of a six-cylinder, turbocharged diesel which was beautifully smooth and quiet compared with the more 'agricultural' four-cylinder units in other vehicles. Sadly at only 2.4 litres it had difficulty pulling the skin off the proverbial rice pudding, and there were other mechanical shortcomings which marred an otherwise superb product which undoubtedly moved the whole minibus market up a gear. It also offered options of automatic gearboxes and power steering, although VW's

non-powered steering was pretty light to start with.

MCW's approach was different again. The Metrorider was built from scratch as a purpose-built psv; although Optare modified the chassis for the CityPacer to make it more suitable for psv operation it was still nonetheless a VW LT-series chassis at heart.

MCW came a bit nearer to restoring the line of psv development. The engine was still at the front, but four- and six-cylinder engines from Cummins or Perkins were offered with or without turbocharging. Automatic gearboxes were offered, though at first manual versions were available. The brakes were more like real bus brakes, in that they were worked by compressed air, and construction was integral. Later, disc brakes were fitted. It was again styled as a bus, not a converted van, though it didn't have quite the panache of the trail-blazing Optare. Both sold very well, particularly to big operators. Yet as a passenger there was just the danger that the essential minibus quality was being lost; there wasn't quite the 'cosiness' of a 16-seater, the driver seemed that bit more remote – but there was at least a bit more room, entrances were wider and steps were lower.

Thus just after deregulation the 25-seater was now considered the 'thing'. Demand for Sherpas virtually died, despite Carlyle coming up with a new purpose-built body for it rather than a converted parcel van. A few operators stayed loyal to the Transit, notably Transit Holdings which developed a new style of Transit body on the new-style chassis cowl, built by Mellor and used extensively by Devon General and the group's later offshoots in Oxford and London. It was taller than most Transits, and looked like an ice cream van, but inside it was pleasantly roomy and light, and only 16 seats were still fitted although the

Above:
Bigger and bigger . . . By the time MCW had widened and stretched the Metrorider it was nearly a full-size bus. This one is Yorkshire Traction 321 (F321 FDT).
D. R. Hall

Below:
The bus reinvented? A Duple-bodied Dennis Dart prototype demonstrates its manoeuvrability in Guildford. *S. Morris*

body could possibly have crammed in another row of seats.

Many fleets stocked up with Ivecos, Renault-Dodges, Optare CityPacers and Metroriders. Yet there was a growing realisation that maybe 25 seats wasn't enough. . . Mercedes was back on the market with its revised models. There was a direct replacement for the 608D in the 609D, which still made quite a good 20-seater. But there were bigger models, the 709D and the 811D and 25-seaters soon appeared on the 709D. But maybe the 811D could offer something bigger – Optare produced a new body on the 811D, a 31-seater, the StarRider. Like the CityPacer before it, the Mercedes front was discarded and the styling was conceived from front to back, rather than stopping short to accommodate a standard bonnet. The Mercedes was rather better endowed with cubic centimetres under the bonnet than the VW too and it soon caught on. Other bodybuilders discovered the potential for bigger minibuses on the new Mercedes. MCW soon came up with an answer, and stretched the Metrorider lengthwise and widthwise, to give a 33-seater – more than twice the capacity of those pioneering Transits! Renault too introduced a bigger version of the old 50-series, the S75, giving seating capacity in excess of the 30 mark. And by the time you had allowed a few standees, 'minibuses' could suddenly accommodate around 40 passengers. London Buses perhaps gave greatest credibility to the minibus when it converted two Routemaster routes, 28 and 31, from 4 March 1989, using Mercedes-Benz 811Ds with 'proper' bus bodies built by Alexanders. These had 28 seats, with

Below:
RF reincarnated? One of the first Wright-bodied Dennis Darts for London Buses is put through its paces in Ballymena prior to delivery. *S. Morris*

room for another 15 standing, a total capacity of 43, about equal with standees, to the decidedly 'un-mini' RF single-decker of the 1950s! They had full-width doorways, proper accommodation for luggage and some single seating around the front end to improve passenger flow. This became London Buses' standard 'minibus', and throughout the country there came a realisation that what was wanted was about 33 seats. Even that arch-Transit fan Transit Holdings bought bigger minibuses, 25-seat Mercedes, though these were to replace full-size buses on longer runs, with the 16-seaters still holding sway in towns. Devon General actually ousted all its big buses before the end of 1990.

There were still problems with minibuses, however big they might have got. They still did not offer quite the amenity of a full-size bus. Throughout the 'minibus revolution' that most traditional of British manufacturers, Dennis, had battened down the hatches, keeping itself going with orders from Hong Kong and by getting into the coach market very effectively with its new Javelin. It had no hope of competing with volume manufacturers such as Mercedes, Ford, Leyland-DAF and Iveco in the van conversion market, but as minibuses got bigger so an opportunity presented itself. Take a vehicle the size of a Mercedes 811, and put the engine at the back out of the way, then all sorts of possibilities are opened up. The entrance, for instance could be ahead of the front wheels, by the driver, with a nice low platform.

Duple produced a very stylish new body for the little 8.5m Dennis, which later passed to Carlyle when Trinity Holdings, parent company of both Dennis and Duple, decided to get out of coach building. Wadham Stringer, Wright and Reeve Burgess all came up with bodies too. London Buses was impressed with the thought of a minibus which looked more like a real bus and ordered it in considerable quantities. Like many larger buses the Dart was designed to have common front and rear modules for all models, with a wheelbase which could be built in several different lengths. First came a 9m option, then a 10m, with up to 43 seats. Here at last was a 'minibus' with a rear engine, automatic transmission as standard, air brakes, power steering, low floor, plenty of headroom, big windows, and options of bodywork with such hi-tech features as bonded panelling and glazing or bolted aluminium construction. And at 10m this 'mini' was only 0.3m shorter than the shorter version of the Leyland National. Carlyle produced a revised body for the 10m version with a door wide enough for a centre handrail, improved access and a full-size destination blind. With 43

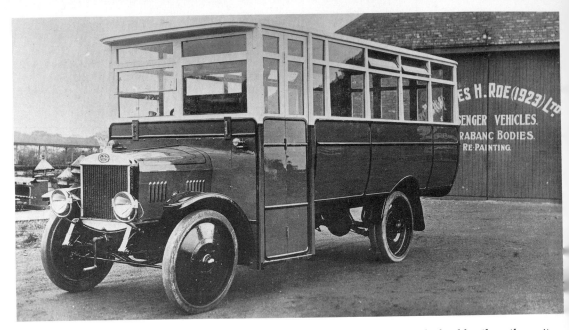

**Nothing new under the sun . . . an early Roe-bodied Guy
14-seater. Would it be unfair to suggest that the Ford
Transits of c1985 showed little development over this? The
Roe factory was later to produce the stylish Optare
CityPacer.** *Ian Allan Library*

seats and 17 standees its capacity was very nearly
the same as the standard double-decker of the
early postwar period, and Carlyle proudly
announced it had developed 'the world's first full-
size midibus'. Dennis's next move was to develop
a new single-decker, based on the Dart layout but
using Javelin running units, built to 11m and
12m lengths. Thus out of 16-seat minibuses has
grown a full-size bus – the bus has been
reinvented!

Below:
**Full circle! Although Transit Holdings is one of the keenest
adherents to the original 16-seat minibus concept, this
Plaxton-bodied Leyland Tiger 53-seater, 997 (F280 HOD) of
its Thames Transit subsidiary must surely be stretching a
point!** *T. Carter*

To readers perhaps a little older than the writer,
this may all sound very familiar. The Transport
Act 1930 limited the size of vehicle which could be
one-man operated to 20 seats, and many a rural
bus route was begun using small buses, perhaps
14-seaters or a bit bigger. These were broadly of
similar layout to the conventional minibus, often
on a chassis derived from a goods chassis. As
demand built up so these were superseded by
vehicles up to about 25 seats, then full-size
single-deckers, which with 35 seats or so were
hardly any bigger than a stretched Metrorider! As
Construction & Use regulations allowed bigger
buses, so full-size buses developed up to about
the size of the 9m Dart – and ultimately up to 36ft
or more. That process took perhaps 40 years; this
time the same process has taken about six years.
Each stage has been billed as a brave, new
development, yet there would seem to be nothing
new under the sun!

Is the real minibus here to stay? The answer
has to be yes; whilst an 8.5m Dart may squeeze
into similar spaces to a Mercedes, a 10m one
probably wouldn't. The more sophisticated
technology takes it away from the original concept
of a low-cost bus both to buy and to run. There
are many routes which do not warrant bigger
capacities, and indeed minibuses are also proving
very useful in keeping some Sunday and evening
services going where the bigger bus used during
the day isn't really needed. But where minibuses
have been very successful in generating traffic it is
inevitable that the old 16-seaters will do
themselves out of a job, as has already proved the
case in many centres throughout the country.